THE
DIRTY
DISHES

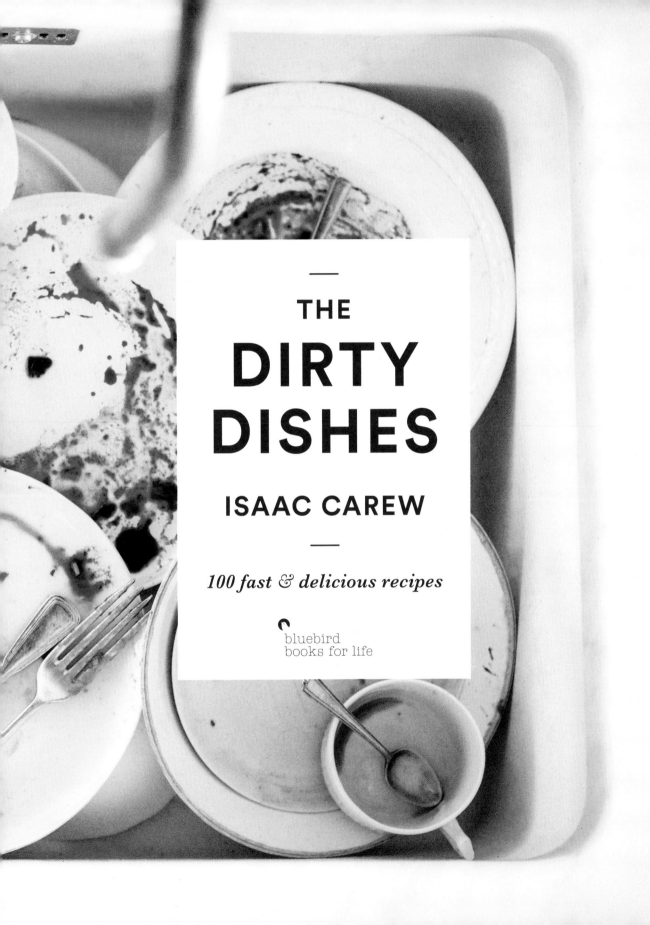

THE
DIRTY
DISHES

ISAAC CAREW

100 fast & delicious recipes

bluebird
books for life

DEDICATION

I'd like to dedicate this book to my mother

The strongest and most wonderful mum:
thank you for raising me the way you have

CONTENTS

contents

contents

"

THE DIRTY DISHES
IS ABOUT COOKING
DELICIOUS, WELL-SOURCED
FOOD AND NOT TAKING IT
TOO SERIOUSLY. YOU NEED
TO BE WILLING TO GET
DOWN AND DIRTY IN THE
KITCHEN – TO TRY SOME
NEW FLAVOURS, TO MAKE
A BIT OF A MESS AND TO
ENJOY EVERY MOMENT.

Isaac Carew

"

INTRODUCTION

The Dirty Dishes

I knew that I wanted to be a chef from a very early age. I grew up in a foodie family and although we didn't have much money, our meals were always the high points of the day and Mum was great at reinventing basic recipes on a budget. Dad was a professional chef and from the age of six I'd sit in the restaurant kitchen and watch him at work, cooking steak and dauphinoise potatoes, making jus or baking amazing eight-layered cakes. But when I wasn't learning the ins and outs of life as a chef, I'd be hanging out with my mates and going to the chicken shop or eating pie and chips. It was a world away from 'fine dining', and these contrasts are still at the heart of my cooking.

I started as a Saturday boy picking spinach leaves when I was just a kid, and after school I trained for two years at catering college. My big break came when, at just eighteen, I landed a job cooking at The Connaught restaurant in London under the legendary chef Angela Hartnett. That's where I really fell in love with cooking: it was so fast-paced and I thrived on the camaraderie of a professional kitchen. It's also where I began my love affair with pasta, which is still one of my favourite things to make and eat.

Everything changed when I was spotted by a modelling scout in my early twenties. Over the next seven or eight years, I put the cheffing on the back burner to focus on modelling. I really missed cooking, but I didn't miss all the late nights working. Modelling also gave me the chance to travel the world: Paris, China, Japan, Mexico. I've experienced a lot of different cultures and, along the way, I've eaten some unforgettable food.

And that's how *The Dirty Dishes* started. I wanted to bring together my favourite dishes, spend some more time in the kitchen and come back to my first love: cooking.

There's an assumption that because I'm a model I'm always super-healthy and live on kale salad. I do work out and eat healthily most of the time, but when it comes to cooking, I'm a chef first and foremost. I love my food and I love the occasional indulgence. Sugar is not off limits; my approach is not about restricting or denying myself (check out my Silly Syllabub on page 224 and Idiot's Eton Mess on page 213). It's also not about being a food snob – I'm just as happy eating someone's nanna's Irish stew as I am having filet steak in a fancy restaurant. For me, food is there to be enjoyed with friends and family.

I've tried to focus on fresh, unfussy food packed with flavours from around the world. But I also want to encourage you to get involved in the kitchen, hanging out with your mates and family and getting your plates dirty with food you love. If you have never cooked before, there are loads of recipes in here just for you, such as my simple Bake-me-up Meatballs (see page 132).

> **"**
>
> *Food should be sociable and the attitude behind* The Dirty Dishes *is to be playful and a little bit cheeky*
>
> **"**

You don't need a fancy cooking technique to enjoy my dishes. Food should be sociable and the attitude behind *The Dirty Dishes* is to be playful and a little bit cheeky (see my Dirty Tomato and Vodka Soup on page 40).

My whole philosophy is to make food that brings happiness. It's all about balance: making food we actually love and finding the time to prepare it. You know what they say, 'A little bit of what you fancy…'? If you're overthinking your food or on a restrictive diet, it is going to make you unhappy. I'm not a nutrition expert, but I know good food and I hope this book will help you eat what you love. Lots of my dishes are based around meat, fish and pasta, but I've also included a vegan chapter in case you want more veg in your diet or you are catering for vegan mates.

And don't worry. Good-quality food doesn't have to cost the earth. Instead of always going to the supermarket, check out local food markets and befriend your local butcher or fishmonger – sometimes they can point you to bargains like a cut of meat that will work hard for your money. The trick is to be savvy and to get to know your food. You don't have to spend an arm and a leg and you're also supporting independent businesses.

Learning how to make simple meals should be back on the agenda. Here's something not a load of people know: I was dyslexic at school, so facts, figures, essays, exams … none of it came easily to me. But I DID know about flavour combinations, spices and the magic of producing a self-crafted plate of food. Food was – and still is – my release, my meditation and my focus. They have stopped teaching kids how to cook at school, but really everyone should know the basics. The more you know, the happier and more connected you are. I want to help people understand that cooking doesn't have to be scary or intimidating. Anyone can do it. You just have to be willing to get your hands dirty, try new things and experiment.

Making great food doesn't have to take up all your time. It shouldn't involve loads of hassle or washing up. If you're relatively new to cooking, I hope this book inspires you to try some new things and to take some time out on a weekend to bake a cake, or whip up a frittata. Get your mates round to eat and kick back with a nice glass of wine. I have a special line in late-night cooking and lazy Sunday brunches, so flick through these pages and get inspired.

Basically my attitude to food is this: eat well, live well and have a bit of fun with it. Let me know how you get on.

Until then, Isaac x

BRUNCH

chapter 1

one-pan scramble

This is a perfect brunch for a hangover, as it's all-in-one and you don't end up with tons of washing up. I'm not a big fan of sausages in a fry-up; you've got so many other great elements in there so I don't think you need them. Small chipolatas work brilliantly here, though.

serves 2

6 rashers of streaky bacon
4 chipolatas
knob of butter
2 large ripe tomatoes, roughly
   chopped, or 8 cherry tomatoes
handful of kale, chopped
sea salt and black pepper
4 medium eggs, whisked
small handful of chives, chopped
pinches of smoked paprika, to serve

Slice the bacon into 2.5cm (1in) pieces and slice each sausage into four pieces.

Heat a large frying pan, add the knob of butter and slide in the meat. Cook for about 8 minutes until golden and brown.

Add the tomatoes to the pan, along with the chopped kale. Fry for 5 minutes, then season with salt and pepper.

Turn the heat down low and stir the whisked eggs into the pan. When the eggs are cooked and just set, remove the pan from the heat. Sprinkle with the chopped chives and a few pinches of smoked paprika. Serve.

buttermilk pancakes with blueberry and chamomile compote

These American-style pancakes are quite a treat. They are also the most calming pancakes you'll ever have because chamomile is known for its soothing qualities. I love blueberries and the chamomile gives a nice floral touch. These are perfect for a relaxed Sunday morning – whack on a bit of classical music and eat these in your dressing gown. The compote takes a bit of time, but it's totally worth it.

makes 6

50g butter, plus extra for frying
150g plain flour
2 tsp baking powder
30g icing sugar
pinch of salt
300ml buttermilk
2 medium eggs
small handful of dried
   chamomile flowers (optional)

FOR THE COMPOTE
4 chamomile tea bags
250g fresh blueberries
1 tbsp honey

First, make the compote. Boil the kettle and measure out 400ml boiling water. Steep the chamomile tea bags for 10 minutes, then squeeze them dry. Add the chamomile water to a medium saucepan along with the blueberries and honey. Cook for about 20 minutes until reduced, syrupy and almost jam-like.

While the compote is reducing, make the pancakes.

Melt the butter. Mix all the dry ingredients in a large bowl. Whisk the buttermilk and eggs together in a jug and, while whisking, slowly pour the mixture into the dry ingredients, followed by the melted butter.

Melt a little butter in a large non-stick frying pan over a medium heat. One small ladleful at a time, pour in the pancake batter – you should be able to make two pancakes at a time.

Cook for 2–3 minutes on each side or until bubbles start to form in the mixture. I always find that the first pancake in the pan is generally a bit of an ugly one! Continue until you have used up all the mixture. You should be able to make about six pancakes from the batter.

Serve the pancakes on two plates, pouring the warm compote over the top. Decorate with a few flecks of chamomile flowers, if using.

cheesy black pudding
hash and eggs

This is a lovely breakfast dish that also works for a midweek dinner because you can use up any leftover potatoes from your Sunday roast.

Hash is a great frugal dish. Food waste is a huge problem and supermarkets don't help – often you can't just buy one onion, you have to buy six and the rest end up going to waste. I always try to use up all my leftovers with dishes like this.

serves 2

400g leftover cooked potatoes,
    roughly chopped, or 2 large (about
    200g) Maris Piper potatoes
sea salt
80g tenderstem broccoli
oil, for frying
100g black pudding
knob of butter
2 medium eggs
100g strong Cheddar cheese

If you need to cook the potatoes, peel and cut them into eighths and place in salted cold water. Bring the water up to boil and cook until tender but not overcooked.

Drain the potatoes, keeping the water. Use the potato water to blanch the broccoli for 2 minutes. Drain.

Heat a glug of oil in a frying pan and fry the potatoes for 5 minutes, or until golden and slightly crisp. Crumble over the black pudding and cook for a few more minutes.

Add the broccoli and a knob of butter. Set aside and let the flavours mix together while you poach your eggs.

Divide the potato mixture between two plates and grate the Cheddar over the top. Top with your poached eggs and serve.

/ *I love poached eggs with this hash*
but you could try fried or scrambled.

bacon and greens fry-up

Yes, this is bacon for brekkie, but halve any guilt because you're getting all your veggies too. I prefer smoked bacon as I think it gives a much better flavour. Always go for good-quality bacon. I think bacon is a bit like whisky – the older you get the more discerning you are about finding the smoke you like! There are so many flavours out there but if I had to choose, I'd go for an oakwood chip smoke.

serves 4

sea salt and black pepper
400g bunch of asparagus,
   woody ends removed
16 rashers of smoked bacon
oil, for frying
250g rosemary sourdough bread
2 garlic cloves, crushed
sweet garlic dressing (see page 237)
handful of lemon balm or parsley
   leaves, roughly chopped

Prepare an ice bath of very cold water in a medium bowl. Bring a large saucepan of salted water to the boil and cook the asparagus for about 2 minutes. Drain and pop straight into the ice bath to cool. This keeps the asparagus a nice and bright colour.

Slice the bacon into bite-sized 2.5cm (1in) pieces. Cook in a large frying pan with a drizzle of oil until golden and crisp. Remove the bacon from the pan but keep the oil for frying the croutons.

Slice and trim off most of the crusts from the sourdough and dice into 2.5cm (1in) pieces. Season with pepper and salt. Fry with the garlic in the bacon oil for about 5 minutes or until golden and crisp.

Toss the croutons, asparagus and bacon together in a large bowl with a drizzle of the sweet garlic dressing. Garnish with the lemon balm or parsley and serve on a big plate.

spinach and goat's cheese muffins

These are great for breakfast on the go and way better than sugar-loaded muffins. Goat's cheese is one of my favourites. When I was about ten years old, my dad used to work at a restaurant in South Kensington. He'd take a huge slab of goat cheese, drizzle it in olive oil and flecks of caraway seed, then grill it with a French baguette. That was my lunch sorted!

makes 6

knob of butter, plus extra
 for greasing
80g baby spinach
sea salt and black pepper
pinch of cayenne pepper
6 medium eggs
2 spring onions, sliced
80g goat's cheese, crumbled
30g Parmesan, grated

Preheat the oven to 180°C (fan 160°C/gas mark 4).

Heat a saucepan with a knob of butter and lightly cook the spinach with a pinch of salt, pepper and the cayenne. Transfer the spinach into a food processor and pulse for 20 seconds, or roughly chop it on a board.

Place the spinach in a medium bowl and whisk in the eggs. Add the spring onions and season with more salt and pepper.

Take a six-hole muffin tin and grease each hole with butter. Divide the mixture evenly between each hole. Top each muffin with the goat's cheese and sprinkle with grated Parmesan. Cook in the oven for 15 minutes, until golden and set.

prawn and chilli
egg white omelette

This is for all the health-conscious out there. Egg whites can be a bit bland by themselves, because you lose the creaminess when you take out the yolk. I've added in the prawns instead because they are so rich in their own way that they add that unctuous depth. This is great post gym when you're really hungry and need something healthy, fast.

serves 1

2 medium egg whites
80g raw king prawns
olive oil, for frying
½ red chilli, deseeded and
    finely sliced
sea salt
juice of 1 lime

Beat the egg whites in a bowl and set to one side. Slice the prawns in half, straight down the middle, making sure to remove any dirt or nasty bits.

Heat a glug of oil in a small frying pan over a high heat. Add the chilli and prawns and fry for 30 seconds. Turn the heat down low, then add the beaten whites and swirl around for about a minute, adding a pinch of salt towards the end. Fold the omelette over with a spatula and fold onto a plate.

Squeeze over the lime juice and serve.

Turkish eggs

I got a bit obsessed with Turkish eggs a few years ago and used to have them nearly every morning. They're great if you've got people round for breakfast because you can do them in a big pan in 6 minutes flat, then serve them, family-style, around the table. They have recently become really big in LA.

serves 4

225g chorizo, chopped into bite-sized chunks
olive oil, for frying
2 red onions, sliced
2 garlic cloves, crushed
1 green pepper, roughly chopped
500ml passata or ½ quantity of basic tomato sauce (see page 244)
sea salt and black pepper
4 medium eggs
bread, to serve (optional)
1 bunch of parsley or coriander, chopped (optional)

Add the chorizo and a glug of olive oil to a large frying pan over a medium heat and cook for a few minutes.

Add the sliced onions to the pan along with the garlic. Fry for a few more minutes, then add the green pepper, along with the passata or tomato sauce. Bring up to the boil, then turn down to a simmer and cook for 6–7 minutes until thickened. Season with salt and pepper.

Make four small wells in the mixture and crack an egg into each one. Season each egg and cover with a lid and cook for about 3–5 minutes, depending on how runny or cooked you like your eggs.

Serve on its own or with some bread and torn parsley or coriander.

SOUPS

chapter 2

beetroot soup with wild garlic scones

This has such a gorgeous colour and a lovely earthy flavour. You can have it hot or cold in summer, just like Russian borscht soup. I opted for scones instead of bread as it's good to mix it up. I've used some of my strong signature flavours. I don't like grey or dull tones – it's all about the bright, vibrant colours.

serves 6–8

1kg beetroot
1 red onion
olive oil, for frying
2 garlic cloves, crushed
1 tbsp brown sugar
2 bay leaves
1–1.5 litres boiling hot chicken
   or veg stock (make your own,
   see pages 52–53)
80ml red wine vinegar
knob of butter (optional)

FOR THE SCONES
(MAKES 6 LARGE OR 12 SMALL)
500g self-raising flour
150g ice-cold butter
1 tsp baking powder
50–100g bunch of wild garlic
   (or use parsley if out of season)
250ml whole milk
2 large eggs, plus 1 extra
   for egg wash
pinch of sea salt

Peel, then top and tail the beetroot. Cut it into rough chunks and set aside.

Roughly chop the red onion and place in a large saucepan with a glug of olive oil. Cook for 3 minutes, then add the crushed garlic, brown sugar and bay leaves. Cook for a further 3 minutes, then add the beetroot. Cover with the stock or the same quantity of boiling water. Cook on a simmer for 30 minutes, adding the red wine vinegar halfway through. Blend until smooth and finish with a large knob of butter for a silkier soup.

While the soup is simmering, make the wild garlic scones. Preheat the oven to 200°C (fan 180°C/gas mark 6). Place the flour and ice-cold butter into a food processor and blend until you have a breadcrumb-like consistency. Transfer the mixture to a bowl and add the baking powder, mixing in with a fork.

Finely chop the wild garlic and add to the bowl.

Whisk together the milk and eggs and slowly add to the flour mixture, until you get a dough consistency. Add the salt.

On a floured surface, roll out the dough until it's roughly 2.5cm (1in) thick or half the size of a cooked scone. Use a pastry cutter to cut out round shapes, or any shape you like. You should be able to make 6–12 scones, depending on the size of your cutter.

Line a baking tray with greaseproof paper. Place the scones on the tray, brush them with a little egg wash and bake for 15 minutes until golden and delicious. Serve the soup with the scones.

carrot and garlic soup

This reminds me of my childhood, because my mum used to make a carrot and coriander version of this when I was growing up. This is my version – the colour of the roasted carrots gives the soup a deep burnished orange colour. This is one of my lighter soups, so it would be good as a starter if you're having people round for dinner.

serves 6–8

1 onion
4 garlic cloves
olive oil, for frying
1 bay leaf
1kg carrots, roughly chopped
sea salt

Roughly slice the onion and crush the garlic cloves. Heat a large pot with a big glug of olive oil and sweat the onions, garlic and bay leaf for 10 minutes.

Add the chopped carrots to the onions and just cover with boiling water. Add a big pinch of salt and cook for 30 minutes until mushy. Blend until smooth and check seasoning. If using a hand blender, always cover the pan with a kitchen cloth to protect you from scalding.

/ You could add butter or crème fraîche for a richer soup, but I like the clean and healthier flavour of just the carrots and seasoning.

chicken and cockle
laksa soup

This will always remind me of my culinary school days in Broadstairs, Kent, and living by the coast. I find cockles are really underused in the UK, and a while back I was inspired to rustle this up when re-watching an old Rick Stein TV episode. What could be better than a surf and turf as a soup, taking you on a culinary journey to the sea?

serves 4

400g chicken thighs,
   cut into strips
sea salt
oil, for frying
200ml coconut milk
300g rice noodles
90g cooked cockles
3 limes
25g coriander

FOR THE PASTE
1 tbsp oil
2 tbsp fish sauce
splash of sesame oil
3 garlic cloves
1 red chilli
1 tsp chilli flakes
1 stick lemongrass
1 thumbnail of ginger
2 tsp ground coriander
1 tsp ground turmeric
1 onion

Add all the laksa paste ingredients into a food processor and blend until you get a smooth silky paste.

Season the chicken with salt. Heat a large saucepan with a big glug of oil and add the chicken. Stir-fry for 3–5 minutes until the meat is slightly golden, then add the laksa paste. Cook for 3 minutes, then add the coconut milk and noodles. Simmer for another few minutes.

Remove the pan from the heat and add the cockles, the juice and zest of two of the limes and the coriander.

Serve in bowls with wedges of the remaining lime.

almond and apple soup

I first had a version of this two years ago on holiday in Mexico. It was so light and delicious and garlicky, I loved it. It's taken me six attempts to perfect this but it was worth it. It might not sound like your normal soup combination, but it works really well. This is perfect for summer, either as a light lunch or an evening starter.

serves 4

250g blanched almonds, plus extra
    for garnish
2 garlic cloves
2 Granny Smith apples, peeled and
    cored, plus 1 extra for garnish
½ cucumber, peeled
250ml good-quality olive oil,
    plus extra to serve
1 tbsp cider vinegar

Add the blanched almonds and garlic to a blender along with a dash of water. Blitz until smooth, then add two of the apples and the cucumber. Add 800ml water and the olive oil and cider vinegar. Whizz for 1–2 minutes, or until smooth and emulsified.

Pop in the fridge for a few hours to get really nice and ice cold. Just before serving, slice the final green apple and chop a few blanched almonds. Garnish each bowl with the apple and almonds and drizzle with olive oil.

/ For smooth soup, use a good-quality, powerful blender. Or blend the soup, then use a ladle to push it through a fine sieve.

dirty tomato
and vodka soup

If you're a vodka fan, you'll love this as it has a serious kick of vodka. It's based on a tomato soup recipe I used to make at The Connaught and I've added an adult, boozy twist. Both the main ingredients really complement each other, you've got the botanical notes from the vodka and the gorgeous red colour of the tomatoes. Zingy, vibrant ... and proof that tomato soup doesn't have to be boring.

serves 6–8

2kg good-quality plum tomatoes
   (don't store them in the fridge)
2 red onions
1 garlic clove, crushed
sea salt
6 black peppercorns
3 glugs of good-quality olive oil, plus
   1 tbsp extra for drizzling
1 bunch of basil, leaves and stalks
   separated
75ml vodka
1 litre hot chicken or veg stock
2 tbsp good-quality balsamic vinegar
toast, to serve

Heat a large roasting tray in the oven at 200°C (fan 180°C/gas mark 6). Meanwhile, cut the tomatoes in half and cut the peeled red onions into quarters. Pop both into a large bowl with the crushed garlic.

Season with a large pinch of salt and the peppercorns. Add three big glugs of olive oil and the basil stalks. Marinate for 10 minutes, or if preparing the day before, marinate overnight for a more intense flavour.

Once the roasting dish is blistering hot, add the bowl of marinated tomatoes and quickly pop back into the oven. Cook for 10 minutes until the tomatoes are slightly burnt and blistered.

Pour the vodka into the roasting dish and cook for another 3–5 minutes in the oven. Add the hot stock and the basil leaves and cook for another 5–10 minutes.

Carefully remove the roasting dish from the oven and either blitz the soup with a hand blender or carefully ladle the soup into a blender and blitz until smooth. If using a hand blender, always cover the pan with a kitchen cloth to protect you from scalding.

Check the seasoning. Drizzle with olive oil and the balsamic vinegar. Serve with some gorgeous, crunchy toast.

roast pumpkin and turmeric soup

My mum and sister are going to laugh when they read this. I had a really bad experience with pumpkin soup when I was young. A family friend was babysitting me and I was forced to eat a bowl of unseasoned pumpkin soup. It was horrible and watery and it put me off pumpkin soup for years. I guess this is my way of making peace with it. The ginger gives an extra kick and I have to say, it's pretty good.

serves 6

1kg pumpkin or butternut squash
olive oil
sea salt
1 tsp ground turmeric, plus extra for top
2 onions
2 garlic cloves
1 stick lemongrass
1 thumbnail of ginger
1–1.5 litres chicken stock (optional)
  (make your own, see pages 52–53)
1 bay leaf

Preheat the oven to 200°C (fan 180°C/gas mark 6). Start by peeling and deseeding the pumpkin or squash. Cut into rough chunks and cover in a glug of olive oil, a pinch of salt and ½ teaspoon of the turmeric. Roast in the oven for 30 minutes.

While the pumpkin is roasting, slice the onions and crush the garlic. Bash the lemongrass and peel and chop the ginger. Heat a large saucepan with a glug of olive oil and fry the onions, garlic, lemongrass, and ginger for 5–8 minutes, until soft, adding the remaining ½ teaspoon turmeric in the last few minutes.

Add the roasted pumpkin to the onion mixture and stir for a couple of minutes, then cover with enough chicken stock or boiling water to just cover the veg. Add the bay leaf and simmer for 30 minutes.

Blitz or blend until smooth. If using a hand blender, always cover the pan with a kitchen cloth to protect you from scalding. Serve drizzled with olive oil and a tiny pinch of turmeric.

roast garlic and white bean soup

This is a lovely, luxurious soup. When you roast garlic you get a sweet, caramelized flavour and it gives great depth to any dish. It's a subtle flavour, rather than being really garlicky (which I don't mind either). This soup is great in the winter because it's heavy and warming. You could eat it as a main meal, along with a couple of slices of bread.

serves 4–6

6 bulbs of garlic
olive oil
sea salt
3 black peppercorns
1 leek, roughly chopped
2 celery sticks, roughly chopped
100g Parmesan rind (see tip)
1 litre vegetable or chicken stock
    (make your own, see pages 52–53)
660g white beans (I like the jars of
    Navarrico beans, which come in
    this quantity, but any tins of white
    beans will work)
6–8 large sage leaves
focaccia, to serve

Preheat the oven to 200°C (fan 180°C/gas mark 6). Cut the tops off the garlic bulbs so just the tips of the cloves are exposed. Cover in a glug of olive oil and salt and wrap in tin foil before placing in the oven to roast for 35–45 minutes until soft and mushy. While these are roasting you can start on the base of the soup.

Heat a deep saucepan with a glug of olive oil. Add the peppercorns and toast for 1 minute. Add the leek and celery and cook for about 8 minutes until soft and translucent. Add the Parmesan rind and the stock. Add the white beans along with the white bean water from the jar or tin, as this will help thicken up the soup. Bring up to the boil, then lower to a simmer.

Take the roast garlic out of the oven and let it cool slightly. Using your fingers and taking care not to burn yourself, push the gorgeous caramelized roasted garlic out of the skins and straight into the soup. Cook for 10 minutes to let the flavours combine. Turn off the heat.

Quickly shallow-fry the sage leaves in olive oil and a pinch of salt until crispy and lightly golden. Remove and place onto a piece of kitchen roll.

Remove the Parmesan rind. Blend the soup until smooth, then check the seasoning and add a pinch of salt and a glug of olive oil.

Serve in bowls topped with the crumbled sage with focaccia on the side.

/ 100g Parmesan rind may seem like quite a lot to have on hand, but I recommend never chucking old rinds away, because they provide so much flavour.

cauliflower and chilli garlic cream soup

This luxurious soup is full of cream and garlic. Be careful it doesn't catch – the first time I made it with milk I ended up burning it at the bottom, so keep an eye on it when you cook it. The cauliflower adds that earthy element. I love black garlic because it's fermented and sticky and has a gorgeous flavour. Always go for good-quality garlic, you'll really notice the difference.

serves 6–8

olive oil, for frying

2 onions or 4 shallots, finely sliced

2 garlic cloves, crushed

pinch of sea salt

2 sprigs of thyme, leaves only

100–200ml white wine

1 large head of cauliflower, chopped

2 litres veg or chicken stock (make your own, see pages 52–53)

FOR THE CHILLI–GARLIC CREAM

2 garlic cloves, chopped

olive oil, for frying

2 tbsp sesame seeds

1 tsp chilli powder

1 tsp smoked paprika

juice of 1 lemon

100ml stock (optional)

100ml single cream

Heat a large saucepan with a glug of oil. Add the onions, garlic and the salt and cook for a few minutes. Add the thyme and cook for 5–8 minutes, or until soft and translucent. Add the white wine and reduce slightly.

Add the chopped cauliflower and simmer for about 10 minutes, covered with a lid. Add the veg or chicken stock and bring to the boil. Simmer for 25–35 minutes. Check the seasoning and blitz in a blender. If using a hand blender, always cover with a kitchen cloth to protect you from scalding.

Blend until smooth, adding a little boiling water if you prefer a thinner texture. Set aside while you make the chilli–garlic cream.

To make the chilli–garlic cream, add the garlic to a small saucepan, along with a glug of olive oil. Sweat for 1 minute, then add the sesame seeds, chilli powder and paprika. Cook for 1 minute on a low heat, seasoning with a pinch of salt. Add the lemon juice and stock or 100ml water. Reduce a little for 2 minutes, then add the cream. Reduce by half (this should take about 3 minutes), until the cream is thick in consistency and bright red.

Heat up the soup and divide between bowls. Drizzle the chilli–garlic cream on top and serve.

fix-me chicken soup

This does exactly what it says on the tin. It's the ultimate feel-good food for when you're feeling a bit tired, or when you get in from work on a Monday night and want something quick and warming. Curling up with a bowl of soup just makes you feel whole. This is more than a hug in a bowl – it's a group hug in a bowl. People have been making chicken soup for centuries; it's proper soul food. You can use any leftover chicken in the fridge from a Sunday roast.

serves 6–8

1 onion
2 celery sticks
1 carrot
1 leek
olive oil, for frying
knob of butter
150g pearl barley
3 garlic cloves, crushed
1 tsp chilli flakes
small glass of cider
2 litres chicken stock (make your own, see page 52)
1 bay leaf
1 head of cavolo nero, leaves torn
300g leftover or pre-cooked chicken, preferably thigh meat
sea salt and black pepper, to season

Slice the onion, celery, carrot and leek into equal-sized chunks.

Heat a large saucepan with a glug of olive oil and a knob of butter. Add the vegetables and the pearl barley and sweat off for a few minutes. Add the crushed garlic and sweat for another 2 minutes.

Add the chilli flakes and 'deglaze' the saucepan by adding the cider and loosening the stuck-on bits on the bottom of the pan with a wooden spoon. Add the chicken stock and bay leaf and bring up to the boil. Simmer for 20 minutes.

Add the torn cavolo nero and chicken and simmer for another 5 minutes. Taste the pearl barley, it should be cooked but still have a little bite to it. Season and serve.

the connaught and angela hartnett's white onion soup

This is a rather decadent winter soup. They have to be decadent in winter, don't they? The recipe uses white onions, which are much sweeter and more delicate than normal ones. Again, be careful that they don't catch when you're cooking them, as you'll end up with a grey-coloured soup instead of a sumptuous white one. This was one of Angela Hartnett's signature dishes when I was working with her and I've made it by the bucketload.

serves 4

1kg white onions

olive oil, for frying

50g butter

2 garlic cloves, halved

1 bay leaf

1 sprig of thyme

1 litre chicken or veg stock (make your own, see pages 52–53)

50–100g crème fraîche

pinch of sea salt

Remove the first layer of each white onion and discard, then slice them as thinly as possible. Heat a large saucepan with a glug of olive oil and melt the butter on a low heat (the olive oil stops the butter from burning).

Add the onions, garlic, bay leaf and sprig of thyme to the pan. Cook for 10–15 minutes on a low heat, constantly stirring so the onions don't catch. You don't want even the slightest bit of colour. Once the onions are translucent, add the chicken or veg stock.

Cover with a lid and cook for 10 minutes. Remove from the heat, remove the thyme sprig, and add the crème fraîche and salt. Blend using a hand blender or food processor until smooth. If using a hand blender, always cover the pan with a kitchen cloth to protect you from scalding.

/ *Veg stock gives you a whiter and brighter soup and is great for vegetarians. The chicken stock gives you a better depth of flavour.*

how to make
basic one-hour
chicken stock

Making stock is a great way of using leftovers. Make this gorgeous chicken stock with the carcasses from your Sunday roast.

makes
2 litres

2 carrots
2 leeks
1 bulb of garlic
2 large chicken carcasses
2 onions, halved
1 bay leaf
3–5 black peppercorns
1 bunch of parsley, stalks only
(optional)

Start by peeling the carrots, then top and tail them and slice vertically down the middle. Cut the leeks vertically down the middle but keep the stems attached. Cut the bulb of garlic in half so the cloves are exposed.

Add the chicken carcasses to a very large saucepan, then pile all of the veg on top. Pour 4 litres of cold water over the top, then add the bay leaf, peppercorns and parsley stalks, if using.

Bring the cold water up to the boil, then reduce down to a simmer and cook for 1 hour, removing any scum or excess fat with a ladle.

Place a colander over a bowl or another large saucepan. Pour the stock in the colander and let it drain for a good 10 minutes, so you don't waste any gorgeous stock. Use immediately, refrigerate for up to 5 days or freeze for up to 3 months.

/ *Make sure you use cold water and bring it up to the boil in the saucepan rather than using water boiled in the kettle.*

how to make
basic veg stock

I love making stock. The more you make from scratch, the more money you save. It is also more environmentally conscious than using shop-bought because you're reducing on packaging.

<table>
<tr><td>makes
2 litres</td></tr>
</table>

4 carrots, roughly chopped
2 onions, roughly chopped
2 leeks, roughly chopped
4 celery sticks, roughly chopped
3 fennel seeds
1 bay leaf
3 white peppercorns
1 bunch of parsley, stalks only
1 unwaxed lemon, halved

Add all of the veg to a very large saucepan along with the fennel seeds, bay leaf, peppercorns and parsley stalks and cover with 4 litres of cold water.

Bring up to the boil and simmer for 10 minutes then add the lemon. Simmer for a further 3 minutes. Remove from the heat and chill immediately to infuse overnight.

The next day, strain and use immediately. You could also refrigerate for a few days or freeze for up to 3 months.

/ To remove dirt from the leeks, slice down the middle and hold under cold running water.

SALADS

chapter 3

caponata and
quinoa salad

Caponata is a cooked aubergine and tomato salad that's often served alone or with a steak. Here I've served it with quinoa, which I love because it's so easy to make. You have to do a bit more prep with all the chopping for the caponata but it's worth it because it tastes so delicious. I don't think we spend enough time on salads – they're just as worthy of care and attention as any other dish.

serves 4

2 large aubergines
1 tbsp olive oil
sea salt and black pepper
1 onion, finely sliced
1 garlic clove, chopped
200g large ripe tomatoes,
   roughly chopped
handful of green olives,
   de-stoned and halved
30g capers, rinsed
1 tsp smoked paprika
1 tsp soft brown sugar
2 tbsp red wine vinegar
50g pine nuts, toasted
250g pre-cooked quinoa
   or 90g uncooked quinoa

Slice the aubergines into cubes about as big as a thumb – any smaller and they'll shrink when cooked. Heat a large saucepan with the olive oil and add the aubergines. Season with salt and pepper and cook for 8–10 minutes or until soft. Drain into a colander or onto a piece of kitchen roll.

In the same pan, add the onion and garlic, season and cook for a few minutes. Add the tomatoes and cook for 1–2 minutes, then add the olives, capers and smoked paprika. Cook down for 5–10 minutes, then add the aubergine back into the pan with the sugar and vinegar. Cook for a further 5 minutes, then remove from the heat.

Stir through the toasted pine nuts, then leave to one side so the flavours have a chance to combine while you reheat the quinoa or cook it according to packet instructions. Divide the quinoa between four plates and top with the caponata.

fennel, orange
and halloumi salad

This is my twist on the classic Greek salad. I'm not a fan of fennel when cooked, but I love it raw, because the aniseed flavour is a lot more subtle and you don't feel as if you're eating a mouthful of liquorice! I also love squeaky, salty halloumi cheese. You can do anything with it and it doesn't lose its shape; it's a good cheese for grilling on the barbecue in the summer for that outdoor vibe.

serves 2–3

1 orange
1 fennel bulb
250g halloumi
olive oil, for brushing
classic vinaigrette, for dressing
  (see page 236)

Top and tail the orange. Slide your knife down and around to remove the skin and pith, then slice into rounds and transfer to a medium bowl.

Slice the fennel down the middle and remove the core and woody tips. Shave the trimmed fennel head using a mandoline or slice as thinly as possible with a sharp knife. Add it to the oranges and toss lightly so the orange juice stops the fennel from oxidizing.

Heat a large griddle pan or frying pan. Slice the halloumi and brush very lightly in olive oil. Fry the slices for a few minute on on each side until charred but not burnt.

Lay the halloumi slices on a large serving plate, then dress the salad with classic vinaigrette and serve.

my godmother's rice salad

This takes me back to when I was fourteen and my godparents were looking after me one summer holiday. My godmother used to make this salad, and I have such a vivid memory of eating it in Greenwich Park and going to see the Royal Observatory there. It's such a simple salad but the rice makes it more substantial: great to make for a party or if you've got a group coming round.

serves 6

350g rice
pinch of sea salt
6 plum tomatoes, cut into four pieces
25g parsley, plus extra for garnish
225g green beans
1 head of chicory, cored and cut into
    four pieces
classic vinaigrette, for dressing
    (see page 236)
2 garlic cloves, crushed
micro herbs, to garnish (optional)

Add the rice to a saucepan over a medium heat with a pinch of salt. Pour over 700ml boiling water and cover with a lid. Cook the rice for 8–10 minutes until light and fluffy. Transfer onto a large plate to cool slightly.

While the rice is cooling, place another saucepan of salted water on to boil. Place the tomatoes in a large bowl. Roughly chop the parsley and add to the tomatoes.

When the water is boiling, top and tail the green beans and cook for 3 minutes. Drain and place them in an ice bath to cool and to keep their vibrant green colour. Add the beans to the tomatoes along with the chicory. Dress with the vinaigrette and crushed garlic.

Mix with the slightly cooled rice and top with more parsley or micro herbs, if using.

A big salad:
the best thing
for feeding
a crowd

my favourite
simple salad

Sometimes the best things in life are the simple things. This salad only has three main ingredients: cherry tomatoes, rocket and aged balsamic vinegar, but takes no time to make and always goes down really well. It's great as a side salad for serving with steak and pasta dishes and is perfect for chucking on the table at a dinner party.

serves 2

8 cherry tomatoes
pinch of sea salt
3 tbsp best-quality extra-virgin olive oil
1 tbsp aged balsamic vinegar
70g rocket

Slice the cherry tomatoes in half with the stem side facing away from you. Pop into a bowl and add the salt, oil and vinegar. Gently mix in the rocket and serve.

*/ You could also add a few shavings
of Parmesan cheese.*

black pudding
and apple salad

When I was a kid I always thought black pudding was gross, but when I started working in kitchens, another chef was making it for breakfast one morning. He offered me some and my reaction was 'No way!' – but then I tried it and the incredible flavour just hit me. I love this one because you have the naughtiness of the black pudding along with the freshness of the salad.

Heat a little oil in a frying pan over a high heat and crumble in the black pudding. Cook for 3 minutes until the meat is golden and crisp. Remove with a slotted spoon and place on a piece of kitchen roll to drain off some of the fat.

Pop a saucepan of water on to boil. Drop the white wine vinegar into the boiling water and crack the eggs in gently. Poach the eggs for a couple of minutes and when cooked, use a slotted spoon to carefully transfer to a piece of kitchen roll.

Meanwhile, add the apple slices to a large bowl, dressing with a little vinaigrette to stop them from oxidizing and going brown. Toast the almonds in a dry frying pan, then remove when slightly golden and leave to cool.

In the same frying pan, add the torn chunks of sourdough, along with the crushed garlic clove and a few glugs of olive oil. Cook until golden.

Add the watercress to the bowl of apples and dress with more vinaigrette and salt. Grab two plates and sprinkle the black pudding liberally over each plate. Then top with the watercress salad, toasted almonds, croutons and poached eggs. Serve.

serves 2

olive oil, for frying
130g black pudding
1 tsp white wine vinegar
2 medium eggs
1 apple, cored and sliced
apple cider vinaigrette, for dressing
  (see page 237)
handful of almonds
2 thick slices sourdough, torn into
  rough chunks
1 garlic clove, crushed
95g watercress
sea salt, to taste

/ Choose a sharp-flavoured apple such as Granny Smith to cut through the fat of the black pudding.

burrata
and beetroot
carpaccio

I love beetroot in any form because it's got great earthy flavour and it's also really good for you. In a modelling career, you pay close attention to detail and appearance and it's the same when it comes to my food. I love how thin the beetroot is sliced here and how the whiteness of the cheese stands out against the bold beetroot.

serves 2–4

2 raw beetroots
1 tbsp classic vinaigrette (see page 236)
1 tsp capers
1 × 200g ball of burrata
70g pea shoots
small handful of walnuts, crushed

Peel and top and tail the beetroots. Thinly slice into rounds (the thinner the better).

Pop the beetroot slices into a bowl and dress with the vinaigrette and capers for a few minutes – the acid from the vinegar will 'cook' the beetroot.

Lay the beetroot on a large plate and place the burrata in the centre. Cut the burrata open in the middle by scoring an 'x' with a knife.

Toss the pea shoots in a little more dressing and add to the plate, then sprinkle with the crushed walnuts and serve.

warm sweet potato
and feta salad

I think sweet potatoes are a bit overrated these days, especially in this health and fitness era. People think real potatoes like Maris Piper are bad for you and sweet potatoes are the Holy Grail – this just isn't true. But they do work really well here with the feta cheese and lemon segments. This dish has got the sweet and sour thing going on; you've got the acidity from the lemons with the sweetness of the potatoes and the saltiness of the feta. You can also wrap up your potatoes in tin foil and cook them on the barbecue.

serves 2–4

2 medium sweet potatoes, peeled
   and cut into 2.5cm (1in) chunks
olive oil
sea salt and black pepper
1 tsp ground coriander
1 lemon
½ red onion, thinly sliced
95g lamb's lettuce
handful of mint leaves
classic vinaigrette, for dressing
   (see page 236)
200g feta cheese, crumbled

Preheat the oven to 220°C (fan 200°C/gas mark 7) and line a large baking tray with greaseproof paper.

Toss the sweet potato chunks in a bowl with a glug of olive oil, a pinch of salt, a few cracks of pepper and the ground coriander. Transfer to the lined baking tray and roast for 20–25 minutes.

While the sweet potatoes are roasting, peel the skin and pith of the lemon, then cut it into four segments and place in a medium bowl. Add the red onion, lamb's lettuce, picked mint leaves and a pinch of salt to the bowl.

Dress with a couple of tablespoons of vinaigrette. Add the cooked sweet potatoes, crumble the feta cheese over the top and stir through one more tablespoon of the dressing. Serve.

spicy and sweet courgette and sultana salad

I love the different textures in this salad: it's all about the chew and crunch. Raw courgettes are so tasty and the spice in the chilli gives them a kick. You've also got the pea shoots for colour and vibrancy, the sultanas for sweetness and the hazelnuts for crunch. I'm a big fan of hazelnuts – they have a much stronger flavour than other nuts and are a great addition to any salad.

serves 2–4

100g sultanas

around 50ml warmed apple juice, for soaking (optional)

2 courgettes

juice and zest of ½ lemon

1 tbsp extra-virgin olive oil

sea salt and black pepper

pinch of chilli flakes

50g blanched hazelnuts

95g pea shoots

handful of parsley, chopped

Place the sultanas in a medium bowl and pour over the warmed apple juice or 50ml warm water. The sultanas should be just covered by the liquid.

Using a vegetable peeler or mandoline, slice the courgettes as thinly as possible. Alternatively you could use a grater. Toss the courgettes with the lemon juice, olive oil, a pinch of salt and the chilli flakes. Allow the acidity from the lemon to 'cook' the courgette.

Meanwhile, toast the hazelnuts lightly in a frying pan, then transfer them to a clean kitchen towel and lightly crush.

Drain the sultanas and add them to the courgettes along with the pea shoots and hazelnuts. Season with salt and pepper and serve garnished with the parsley and lemon zest.

sesame beef, kimchi and red cabbage salad

I first tried kimchi in Korea a few years ago, when I ordered a dish called Shabu Shabu, which is like a Korean version of Japanese ramen. It came with kimchi on the side, and I loved it from the first mouthful. It's spicy and vinegary fermented cabbage and is great for gut health. I can eat a whole bowl of it by itself.

serves 2

200g sirloin steak (or 200g
   leftover roast beef, sliced)
oil, for frying
salt and black pepper
½ red cabbage, cored
   and thinly sliced
1 tbsp sesame oil
juice and zest of ½ lime
80g kimchi
handful of cashews
mint leaves, to serve

If you're cooking the steak, set a frying pan over a high heat until searing hot. Cover the steak in oil, season with salt and pepper and sear for 2 minutes on each side. Remove the steak from the heat and rest for 4 minutes.

Place the sliced red cabbage in a medium bowl with the sesame oil and the lime juice. Add in the kimchi.

Toast the cashews in a dry frying pan and lightly crush or chop them.

Slice the rested steak and mix it through the cabbage and kimchi.

Divide the salad between two plates and cover with picked mint leaves, the crushed cashews and a small grating of the lime zest.

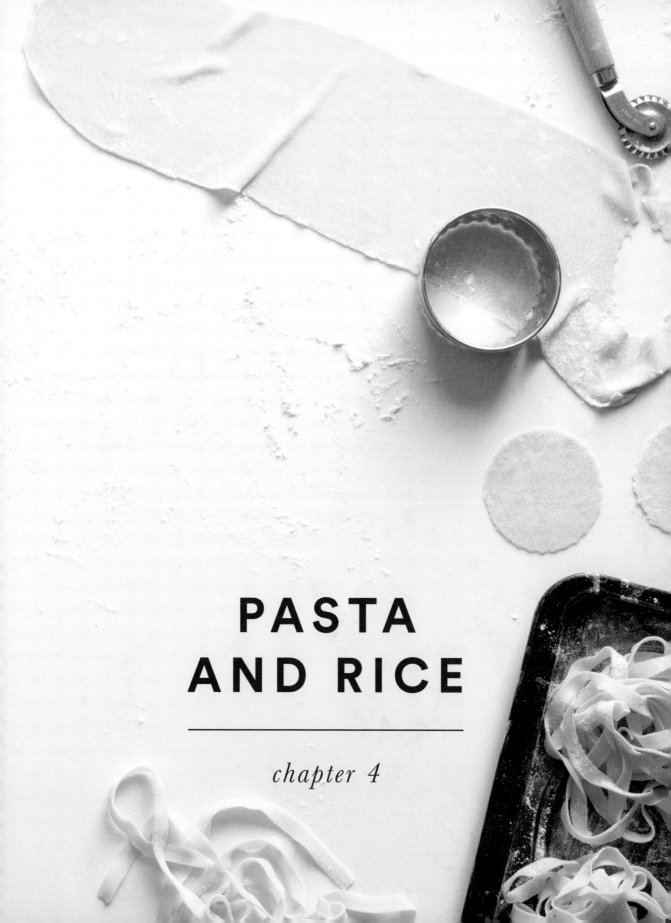

PASTA AND RICE

chapter 4

prawn, lemon and asparagus risotto

I was on the pasta section when I worked for Angela Hartnett at The Connaught, and I recently worked out that I've cooked over 20,000 risottos in my time! I know how they should be cooked: don't rush the process, add a ladle of stock at a time rather than pouring it all in at once, and always add the butter at the end. This simple and fresh risotto was inspired by a 'using-everything-in-my-fridge' kind of night.

serves 4

olive oil

200g cold butter, chopped

2 shallots or 1 small onion,
  finely chopped

1 garlic clove, chopped

400g Arborio risotto rice

200ml white wine

1 litre hot fish or chicken stock

12 king prawns, peeled and
  sliced in half (or see tip)

sea salt

12 asparagus tips

100g Parmesan, finely grated

small handful of chives, chopped

zest of 1 lemon

Add a glug of olive oil and a thumb of butter to a large saucepan, then add the chopped shallots or onion and garlic. Cook for 2–3 minutes over low to medium heat until slightly translucent and sweet. Add the rice and cook for another 2–3 minutes on a low heat.

Turn up the heat to high and pour in the white wine. Bubble until the wine is reduced, then add the hot stock, one ladle at a time, cooking for about 18 minutes or until the rice is al dente. Risotto rice should be cooked within 22 minutes, but always test as you go along.

Around 5 minutes before you wish to serve, heat a large frying pan to searing hot, then add a healthy glug of olive oil. Add the prawns and a pinch of salt and cook for 30 seconds, then add the asparagus tips and cook for a further 30 seconds.

Just before serving, add the prawns and asparagus to the risotto along with the remaining butter, Parmesan, chopped chives and the lemon zest. Serve.

/ *You could slice eight of the king prawns in half and leave four whole for garnishing each plate.*

puréed parsley risotto with mushrooms

Parsley is one of my favourite herbs. It's so versatile and it gives a really clean, simple flavour to dishes. I use it in a lot of things. I love the earthy feel and flavour that you get from the ingredients in this dish. The mushrooms give meaty texture, while the colour of the purée is so eye-catching and vibrant.

serves 4

olive oil, for frying
200g cold butter, chopped
2 shallots or 1 small onion, chopped
400g Arborio risotto rice
150ml white wine
1 litre hot vegetable stock
240g fresh mushrooms (about
    3 large handfuls)
100g Parmesan, grated
sea salt and black pepper

FOR THE PURÉE
1 large bunch of parsley, leaves
    and stalks separated
50–100ml olive oil

First, make the purée. Prepare a bowl of iced water and bring a saucepan of salted water to the boil. Drop the parsley stalks in the water to blanch for 5 minutes, then add the leaves. Boil for 30 seconds, then drain through a colander and transfer to the bowl of iced water.

Drain the parsley again and place it on a clean kitchen towel. Bring up the sides of the tea towel and squeeze any excess water out into the sink. Add the parsley to a blender with 50ml olive oil and blend until smooth. (Add more oil if it needs it – you want a really smooth purée.) Set aside.

For the risotto, add a glug of olive oil and a thumb of butter to a large saucepan, then add the chopped shallots or onion. Cook for 2–3 minutes over low to medium heat until slightly translucent and sweet. Add the rice and cook for another 2–3 minutes on a low heat.

Turn up the heat to high and pour in the white wine. Bubble until the wine is reduced, then add the hot stock, one ladle at a time, cooking for about 18 minutes or until the rice is al dente. Risotto rice should be cooked within 22 minutes, but always test as you go along.

Take the pan off the heat and add the mushrooms (they can either go in raw, or you can fry them for 1 minute in olive oil), remaining butter, Parmesan and parsley purée. Stir well and season with salt and pepper to taste.

sausage and red wine risotto

I imagine this is something a king would sit down to eat – it's so decadent. The flavours from the sausages and the red wine make it really rich. It's like a massive hug in a bowl. Make sure it looks as good as it tastes: don't just slap it out into a dish, but ladle the cooked risotto out carefully and give it a little shake, so it evens out in the bowl and isn't just a lumpy mess.

serves 4

4 Italian sausages
2 shallots or 1 small onion, finely chopped
400g Arborio risotto rice
200ml red wine
1 litre beef or chicken stock
100g Parmesan, finely grated
200g cold butter, chopped
handful of parsley, freshly chopped
handful of sage, freshly chopped

Peel the skin from the sausages and discard. Roughly break the sausage meat into bite-sized pieces, either by hand or with a knife. Fry the sausage meat in a large dry saucepan until slightly crisp, golden and broken up, then remove from the pan using a slotted spoon and set side.

In the same pan, add the chopped shallots or onion and cook in the sausage fat. Cook for 2–3 minutes over low to medium heat until slightly translucent and sweet. Add the rice and cook for another 2–3 minutes on a low heat.

Turn up the heat to high and pour in the red wine. Bubble until the wine is reduced, then add the hot stock, one ladle at a time, cooking for about 18 minutes or until the rice is al dente. Risotto rice should be cooked within 22 minutes, but always test as you go along.

Mix through half the cooked sausage, half the Parmesan and the butter, then take the pan off the heat. Just before serving, top with the remaining Parmesan and cooked sausage, as well as the chopped parsley and sage.

nduja
vongole

The first time I had a vongole was at the famous River Café in London, and it was amazing. Vongole is a classic Italian dish: clams, spaghetti and white wine. I've added a twist and spiced mine up with my beloved nduja. It tastes great and looks lovely on the plate – a great dish if you want to impress your girlfriend or boyfriend.

serves 2

sea salt and black pepper
olive oil
200g linguine
450g clams
30g fresh nduja (or else from a jar)
½ bunch of parsley, roughly chopped
80ml white wine
juice of ½ lemon

Put a medium saucepan of water over a medium heat and bring to the boil, hitting it with a generous pinch of salt and glug of olive oil. When it reaches the boil, pop in the pasta and cook until al dente.

While the pasta is cooking, make sure the clams are nice and clean with no dirt or sand. In a large saucepan, add another glug of olive oil and the nduja and cook for 1 minute. Add the clams, parsley and white wine and cover with a tight-fitting lid.

Shake the pan, then cook with the lid on for 4–5 minutes, or until all the clams have opened up nicely. Chuck any away that are still closed, as these will be no good.

Drain the pasta and add it straight to the pan of clams, adding salt, pepper, another glug of olive oil and the lemon juice. Serve.

nduja tagliatelle

I've had a proper love affair with nduja for about two years now. It's an Italian spreadable salami that gives any dish a massive kick. It's packed with herbs and spices, while adding a gorgeous red colour. I can't see my love for nduja stopping any time soon; it's really easy to use and you can add it to anything.

serves 4

olive oil, for frying
1 onion, chopped
100g fresh nduja (or else from a jar)
100–200ml white wine (1 large glass)
1 × 400g tin of chopped tomatoes or
   400g fresh cherry tomatoes, chopped
400g fresh or dried tagliatelle
sea salt
handful of fresh basil leaves, torn
80–100g Parmesan, grated

Heat a glug of olive oil in a frying pan and add the chopped onion. Cook over a low to medium heat for 3 minutes, stirring with a wooden spoon. Add the nduja, trying to break it up as much as possible with the spoon in the pan, and cook for another 2 minutes.

Turn up the heat to medium then add the white wine. Allow the mixture to reduce by half (about 3–4 minutes), then add the chopped tomatoes. Allow the mixture to reduce again, until you reach a sauce-like consistency (about 5–8 minutes).

I love using fresh tagliatelle for this dish but dried works just as well. Bring a saucepan of salted water to the boil, and drop in the pasta. Cook for 1 minute or according to packet instructions until al dente.

Remove the pasta from the water, reserving 1–1½ ladles of the pasta water. Mix the pasta with the nduja sauce and the reserved water.

Serve with torn basil and the grated Parmesan.

/ Mixing the reserved pasta water through the tagliatelle gives it a nice gloss.

crab linguine

Crab is quite an underused ingredient. I think a lot of people try brown crab meat first and don't like it, or find a whole crab a daunting challenge. But it's actually very easy to cook and the combination of crab and chilli creates a clean-tasting but fiery dish. I nearly always choose linguine over spaghetti – sauces cling to linguine easily and you get more from every mouthful.

<table>
<tr><td>serves 4</td></tr>
</table>

sea salt
olive oil
1 shallot, finely chopped
2 garlic cloves, chopped
½ medium red chilli, sliced (see tip)
1 sprig of thyme, leaves only
100ml white wine
1 × 400g tin of chopped tomatoes
360g linguine
100g white crab meat
1 tbsp mascarpone
juice of ½ lemon
a few chives, finely chopped, to serve

Whack a saucepan of salted water on to boil. In the meantime, heat a medium frying pan over a low to medium heat, add a little olive oil and sauté the shallot and garlic until sweet and tender.

Add the chilli to the pan, along with the thyme leaves and cook for a few minutes. Next add the white wine and cook over a medium heat for another minute or two until the sauce is reduced. Finally add the chopped tomatoes and simmer for 5 minutes.

Chuck the linguine in the salted boiling water and cook until al dente. Retaining 1–1½ ladles of the pasta water, strain the pasta and set aside.

Add the crab meat and mascarpone to the sauce, then fold the sauce through the pasta, adding the reserved water. This will give extra gloss to the dish and a deeper taste. Finish with a little drizzle of olive oil, the lemon juice and a sprinkling of chives.

/ Do a taste test to see how spicy your chilli is. If it's too hot you can remove the seeds and just use the flesh.

my simple bolognese

Three different influences combine for this dish. Growing up, I used to make a bog-standard American-style Bolognese – your basic tomato sauce with beef mince. When I started working for Angela Hartnett, I learned to use different types of meat, for instance diced veal instead of mince, and to cook it with a lot more love and care. Finally, the mum of an ex used to bake her Bolognese in the oven, which gave it a great crust on top and that delicious, almost burnt flavour. The result is this simple, winning Bolognese.

serves 4

olive oil
2 celery sticks, chopped
1 onion, chopped
1 garlic clove, chopped
250g veal mince
250g beef mince (at least
   12% fat content)
sea salt and black pepper
2 tbsp tomato purée
200ml red wine
400g chopped tomatoes
   (tinned or fresh)
400ml chicken stock
3–4 bay leaves
5 sprigs of thyme
400g spaghetti
a few basil leaves
100g Parmesan, grated

Heat a glug of olive oil in a large, deep ovenproof saucepan over a low to medium heat. Add the chopped celery, onion and garlic and cook for 5 minutes, then remove from the pan and set aside.

Add a little more oil to the pan, then add both kinds of mince. Season with salt and pepper and brown the meat for about 5 minutes (add in two batches if your pan isn't big enough), then add the celery, onion and garlic back into the pan, along with the tomato purée. Cook for a further 2 minutes.

Preheat the oven to 180°C (fan 160°C/gas mark 4). Add the red wine and cook for about 3 minutes to allow it to evaporate, then add the chopped tomatoes and stock. Add the bay leaves and thyme sprigs.

Continue to simmer for 5 minutes, then place the pan in the oven for 1 hour, until there is a golden layer on top and the sauce is nicely thick.

Cook the pasta in boiling salted water according to packet instructions and serve topped with the Bolognese, torn basil leaves and the grated Parmesan.

aubergine ravioli

I got the inspiration for this from a meal I had at a tiny restaurant in Venice. I don't even remember the name of the place, but it had a daily menu with amazing food. Aubergine has a very meaty texture and is a good alternative if you want to go meat-free. I lived on pasta and Aperol Spritz when I was in Venice – they go surprisingly well together!

serves 4

1 quantity of basic pasta dough
  (see page 114)
olive oil
1 onion, finely sliced
2 smoked garlic cloves, chopped
1 garlic clove, chopped
2 aubergines, diced
1 tbsp dried oregano
100–200ml white wine
4 tbsp good-quality balsamic vinegar
sea salt and black pepper
handful of parsley, finely chopped
1 quantity of basic tomato sauce
  (see page 244)

SPECIAL EQUIPMENT
pasta machine
7cm (2¾ in) round cutter

/ If you want you could plunge the cooked ravioli straight into an ice bath (a bowl with water and ice cubes) to halt the cooking, then reheat when ready to serve.

Make the pasta dough according to instructions on page 114. While it's resting, make the aubergine filling.

Heat a medium saucepan and add a big glug of olive oil. Cover and sweat the onion and both types of garlic for 5 minutes, then add the diced aubergines. Leave the lid off and cook down for 10–15 minutes before adding the oregano and the white wine.

Turn up the heat to high and reduce until the wine has evaporated, then add the balsamic vinegar. Cook for a further 5 minutes, then add 1 tablespoon of olive oil and remove from the heat. Season with salt and pepper.

Pop the aubergine mixture into a food processor and pulse until you have a slightly coarse paste – you don't want it too smooth. Add the chopped parsley right at the end. Transfer to a bowl and chill in the fridge for 20 minutes while you make the basic tomato sauce (see page 244).

Follow the instructions on page 114 to roll out your pasta to the thinnest setting with a pasta machine. Use the cutter to cut out twenty-four rounds of the pasta.

Lay out twelve of the pasta rounds on a floured surface. Spoon out 1 tablespoon of the chilled aubergine mixture and roll it on the edge of the bowl to form a rough ball. Place the mixture in the centre of a pasta round, then repeat with the other eleven rounds.

Brush some egg mixture (leftover from the pasta dough) around the edges of the pasta round, then press an unfilled round on top, sealing each ravioli with your finger and thumb. Press down to release any excess air.

Reheat the tomato sauce and bring a large saucepan of salted water to the boil. Drop the ravioli into the boiling water for 1 minute, then drain and serve immediately, topped with the tomato sauce.

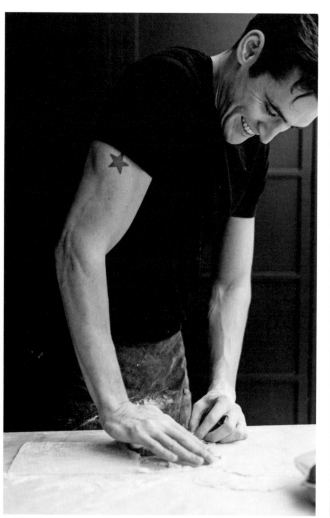

potato gnocchi with burnt butter sauce

This is what I call 'peasant food', because it's basically made from potato and flour. People think making gnocchi is hard but it's actually very simple. The trick is not to overthink it and don't mess around too much when you're making it – you want a lightly cooked cloud rather than a soggy wet pillow. The burnt butter adds a nutty background against the sharpness of the capers.

serves 2

450g Maris Piper potatoes, peeled and quartered
50–100g grade Tipo '00' flour
grating of nutmeg
sea salt
1 small egg
50g Parmesan, grated

FOR THE SAUCE
150g unsalted butter
1 tbsp sherry vinegar
150ml chicken stock
1 tbsp baby capers
few sprigs of chives, chopped

SPECIAL EQUIPMENT
potato ricer

Place the potatoes in a large saucepan of cold, salted water and bring up to the boil, then simmer for 15 minutes until the potatoes are soft but still have a little bite. Drain them and leave to stand for 1–2 minutes until they stop steaming.

Put the potatoes through a potato ricer straight onto a clean, floured surface. Grate a little nutmeg over the top and season with salt. Dust with 50g flour and whisk in the egg, mixing the dough together quickly but lightly. If the dough is a little wet, add a bit more flour.

When you have the dough, roll it into a cigar shape, then cut into thumb-sized portions and set aside.

For the sauce, add the butter to a medium saucepan and cook until it starts to turn golden and smell nutty. Add the vinegar and chicken stock, whisk together for 2 minutes to form an emulsion. You could also use a blender to do this step if you prefer. Stir through the capers and chives.

When you're ready to serve, bring a large saucepan of water to the boil. Drop in the gnocchi pieces for 1 minute, then drain and serve immediately with the caper sauce and grated Parmesan.

/ If you're making ahead, you could plunge the cooked gnocchi straight into an ice bath (a bowl with water and ice cubes) to halt the cooking, then reheat when ready to serve.

butternut squash cannelloni

This is a classic, hearty winter dish that's perfect when cooking for a crowd – it involves quite a few stages but it's actually a very straightforward process. The most technical part is rolling out the cannelloni, but don't overthink it; just get rolling. The finished result is very impressive and makes it look as if you really know what you're doing!

serves 6–8

1 large butternut squash, peeled, deseeded and cut into chunks

2 tbsp olive oil, plus extra for frying

sea salt and black pepper

1 tsp cayenne pepper

1 quantity of basic tomato sauce (see page 244)

100g burrata, chopped or torn

100g Parmesan, grated

300g baby spinach

300g fresh lasagne sheets

grating of nutmeg

40g parsley, finely chopped

Preheat the oven to 200°C (fan 180°C/gas mark 6). On a roasting tray, cover the chopped squash in the olive oil. Add a large pinch of salt and the cayenne pepper. Bake in the oven for 30 minutes, until the squash is soft and slightly golden and crisp around the edges. Meanwhile, make the basic tomato sauce (see page 244) and set aside.

Lower the oven temperature to 180°C (fan 160°C/gas mark 4). Transfer the squash to a chopping board and when cool enough to touch, roughly chop to a fairly coarse mixture. Transfer to a medium bowl and stir through the burrata and half of the Parmesan.

Add a small amount of olive oil to a saucepan and add the spinach. Add salt and pepper and a dash of water and sauté for 30 seconds, until the spinach wilts – don't cook for longer than 2 minutes. Set aside.

Bring a saucepan of salted water to the boil and drop in the lasagne sheets for 1 minute. Remove and lay out flat, one by one, on a clean kitchen towel.

On each sheet, spread a spoonful of the butternut squash mixture and a small layer of spinach. Roll it up like a cigar, then cut in half widthways. Repeat until you run out of mixture or pasta sheets. Grease a thick-bottomed tin or roasting tray – depending on size, you may need two.

Place the cannelloni in the tin. Drizzle with olive oil and most of the remaining Parmesan and a grating of nutmeg. Cover with a lid or a sheet of tin foil and cook in the oven for 15 minutes. Remove the lid and bake for another 5 minutes, while reheating the tomato sauce.

Layer the hot tomato sauce on each plate and place the cannelloni on top. Sprinkle with parsley and the leftover Parmesan and serve.

farfalle with red pepper pesto

This is an easy, go-to recipe when you get in from work and you've got a jar of roasted peppers in the cupboard. Either mash up the peppers in a blender, or chop by hand to make the pesto, then cook the pasta. It's a simple, quick dinner that's also really tasty. Farfalle pasta is good to use in 'saucy' recipes because it scoops up the liquid really well.

serves 6–8

large handful of blanched almonds
500g fresh red peppers (or use 2 jars of roasted red peppers, drained)
80g Parmesan
2 garlic cloves
olive oil
sea salt
500g farfalle (70–80g per person)

TO SERVE
zest and juice of 1 lemon
handful of rocket
pinch of chilli flakes
handful of basil leaves

Gently toast the almonds in a dry frying pan over a low heat until golden but not burnt. Set aside and cool.

Now for the peppers. You can use jarred peppers to save time, but I like to chargrill them myself. Preheat the oven to its lowest temperature. Start by blowtorching the peppers, or heating them on a naked gas burner until the skin is burnt and black. To blowtorch safely, try sticking a fork into the stem of the pepper or put them on a heatproof tray.

Place the peppers in a heatproof bowl, cover with good-quality cling film and place in the oven for 1 hour. Afterwards, run the peppers under a tap to remove seeds and excess skin.

Chuck the peppers into a blender along with the almonds, Parmesan and garlic. Add a huge glug of olive oil and a pinch of salt and blend until smooth.

Bring a medium saucepan of salted water to the boil and cook the farfalle according to packet instructions until al dente.

Stir the pesto through the cooked farfalle with the lemon zest and juice, and garnish with the rocket, chilli flakes and basil.

/ This pesto is also delicious spread on toasted sourdough or ciabatta.

broccoli and egg yolk spaghetti

I first made this dish when I came home drunk and hungry from a night out. I put the spaghetti on to boil, then blanched the broccoli and added the egg yolk to the cooked pasta at the end. It tastes lovely and it's only got three ingredients, so super easy. It's a good alternative to a bacon sarnie if you want to soak up the booze – you've got your carbs and protein there, as well as your healthy veg. Just make sure you don't cook the eggs for too long – you don't want to end up scrambling them.

serves 4

6 medium eggs
400g spaghetti
olive oil, for frying
4 garlic cloves, finely sliced
sea salt and black pepper
1 tsp chilli flakes
2 heads of broccoli (florets only)
handful of chopped watercress
50–100g Manchego cheese, grated

Start by separating the egg yolks from the whites (save the whites to make another recipe such as the egg white omelette on page 28). Set aside.

Bring a medium saucepan of salted water to the boil and add the spaghetti.

Heat 2 large glugs of the olive oil in a large saucepan, then add the sliced garlic, a pinch of salt and the chilli flakes. Cook for 4 minutes, then add the broccoli florets, along with a ladle of the pasta water. Cook for a few minutes.

Once the spaghetti is al dente, add to the broccoli. Remove from the heat, then stir through two egg yolks, another ladle of pasta water, the chopped watercress and Manchego cheese. Portion into four bowls and place another egg yolk on top of each portion – the heat from the pasta will cook it and give you a lovely silky texture and rich flavour. Season and serve.

fusilli with fresh
basil pesto

Basil pesto is a kitchen staple for me. I make it at least twice a week. It's so easy to make and you can use it to add flavour to so many things; you can even spread it on a pizza base. This pesto brightens up any dish. I've suggested fusilli pasta because all the sauce soaks into the texture of the pasta and gives a more intense flavour.

serves 4

sea salt
400g fusilli
2 garlic cloves
50g pine nuts, toasted
olive oil
1 large bunch of basil, leaves only
juice and zest of ½ lemon
50g Parmesan, grated
2 medium eggs

Bring a medium saucepan of salted water to the boil and add the fusilli. Cook according to packet instructions until al dente.

Meanwhile, make the pesto. Crush the garlic in a pestle and mortar and add the toasted pine nuts. Add a little olive oil and continue to crush until it becomes a paste. Reserving a few basil leaves for garnish, add the basil leaves to the mix, along with the lemon juice – this helps to keep the colour green and vibrant. Stir through most of the grated Parmesan. Add more or less olive oil, depending on how thick you want the pesto to be.

In a small bowl, separate the egg yolks from the whites (save the whites for another recipe such as the egg white omelette on page 28).

Put the egg yolks in a large bowl and stir through the pesto. Tip the cooked pasta into the bowl, along with a ladle of the pasta water. Stir through and serve with the lemon zest, a few torn basil leaves and the remaining grated Parmesan.

/ If you prefer you could use
a blender to make the pesto.

carbonara
bucatini

Everyone loves a carbonara, right? I used to make it as a kid and use loads of double cream – I was kind of blown away when I realized that the traditional Italian method of making carbonara doesn't use cream. It's so much better without it: you can taste all the flavours. To change it up I'm using bucatini, but you can go traditional with spaghetti.

serves 4

8 medium eggs
400g fresh or dried bucatini pasta
olive oil
2 garlic cloves, lightly crushed
200g fresh pancetta, diced
100g Parmesan, grated, plus extra
  for serving
sea salt and black pepper

Bring a saucepan of salted water to the boil. In a small bowl, separate the egg yolks from the whites (save the whites for another recipe such as the egg white omelette on page 28).

Add the pasta to the boiling water and cook according to packet instructions until al dente.

Meanwhile, add a small glug of olive oil to a large frying pan, then add the garlic cloves. Cover and sweat without allowing the garlic to colour, then add the diced pancetta. Cook until golden and crisp and the fat has been rendered, around 5–8 minutes.

Remove the pan from the heat and crush the garlic into a paste if soft enough, or discard. Drain the pasta, reserving 1–1½ ladles of the pasta water.

Stir the cooked pasta, egg yolks, grated Parmesan, a small pinch of salt and pepper and the pasta water into the frying pan.

Spoon it onto serving plates and finish with a small grating of Parmesan and more pepper.

mushroom and burrata tagliatelle

I'm not a huge fan of mozzarella, but burrata is life-changing. Seriously. When you cut it open and the middle oozes out, all that creamy, delicious goodness ... I love it. It makes any sauce extra-special. Mushrooms are always good in pasta dishes too, because they add meaty texture.

serves 4

400g tagliatelle
olive oil, for frying
500g girolle (chanterelle) mushrooms, lightly cleaned (see tip)
small knob of butter
1 garlic clove, crushed
8–10 black olives, halved
8–10 green olives, halved
2 large vine-ripened tomatoes, chopped
2 balls of fresh burrata, torn into bite-sized pieces
juice of ½ lemon
handful of chives, chopped
sea salt and black pepper

Bring a saucepan of salted water to the boil. Cook the tagliatelle according to packet instructions until al dente.

Meanwhile, heat a glug of olive oil in a large frying pan and add the mushrooms. Cook on a very high heat for 1 minute, then add the butter, along with the garlic, olives and chopped tomatoes. Cook for another 2–3 minutes, until the tomatoes have turned slightly mushy and more sauce-like.

Drain the pasta, reserving 1–1½ ladles of the pasta water. Add the reserved water to the mushrooms in the frying pan, then stir through the pasta, burrata, lemon juice, chopped chives and a crack of pepper. Serve.

/ *To clean the mushrooms, fill up your sink with cold water and dunk mushrooms lightly – you don't want to bruise them. Allow to dry on a piece of kitchen roll.*

'all the veg' pasta bake

This is so easy and gives you all your daily veg in one dish. It's also great for serving to big groups of people. Take a big pan, chuck in all your leftover veg from the fridge and put it in the oven. You can leave it to cook while you go and watch TV or chill out.

serves 4–6

400g rigatoni pasta
olive oil
1 red onion, finely chopped
2 garlic cloves, crushed
25g bunch of basil, stalks and leaves separated
1 aubergine, cut into bite-sized pieces
1 red pepper, cut into bite-sized pieces
1 courgette, cut into bite-sized pieces
1 litre passata or 1 quantity of basic tomato sauce (see page 244)
1 × 400g tin of chopped tomatoes
sea salt and black pepper
100g Cheddar cheese, grated

Bring a large saucepan of salted water to the boil. Cook the rigatoni according to packet instructions, but remove the pan from the heat 2–3 minutes before the pasta is cooked.

Heat a glug of olive oil in a large ovenproof frying pan and fry the onion and garlic for a few minutes, then add the basil stalks and all of the chopped veg. Cook for a few minutes, then add the passata or tomato sauce and chopped tomatoes.

Preheat the oven to 200°C (fan 180°C/gas mark 6).

Drain the cooked pasta and add it to the veg pan. Give it a good stir to mix everything together. Season with salt and pepper and dot all the basil leaves in and around the mixture. Top with the Cheddar cheese and cook in the oven for 35–45 minutes until all the veg are cooked.

Just before serving, drizzle the bake with another glug of olive oil.

rabbit maltagliati

This is one of my more 'cheffy' dishes. It takes a lot of care and is quite technical but the results are worth it. Rabbit meat is used a lot in France and Italy, but we don't really eat a lot of it here. It's actually a great choice if you fancy something different: it's relatively cheap and has a lovely rich flavour. It works really well with the maltagliati, which are basically the cut-off pieces left over from making pasta.

serves 2

75g pancetta, diced
olive oil, for frying
2 rabbit legs
sea salt and black pepper
1 onion, finely diced
1 celery stick, finely diced
2 garlic cloves, crushed
1 bay leaf
1 × 125ml glass of red wine
100ml hot chicken stock (optional)
1 sprig of rosemary
250g maltagliati pasta
75g breadcrumbs
a few thyme sprigs, leaves only

Add the diced pancetta to a cold, large frying pan with a glug of olive oil and bring up to a high heat. Cook the pancetta until golden and crisp. Remove from the pan and set aside, leaving the pancetta oil in the pan.

Season the rabbit legs and fry them in the pan over a medium heat for 1 minute on each side to seal the meat. Set the sealed legs aside and add the onion, celery, garlic and bay leaf to the pan. Fry for a few minutes.

Turn down the heat and add the rabbit legs back into the pan. Add the wine and bring up to the boil, then add 100ml of boiling water or hot chicken stock. Add a sprig of rosemary and cover with a lid. Cook on a low simmer for 35–45 minutes until the rabbit meat begins to fall off the bone.

Remove the rabbit from the pan, saving all the juices. Pick off all the meat and chuck away the bones. Shred the meat with a fork.

Strain the sauce and add it back to the pan with the rabbit meat.

Bring a large saucepan of salted water to the boil and cook the maltagliati pasta according to packet instructions until al dente.

Meanwhile, add the pancetta and breadcrumbs to a blender, along with the thyme and a pinch of salt. Blend and set aside.

Serve the pasta in two bowls, topped with the pancetta breadcrumb mix.

dirty lasagne

This is one of my trademark dishes and it's super easy and delicious. It's more dirty than your average lasagne, because I load up with cheese and never skimp on the sauce. It's a rich, tasty dish that is there to be enjoyed. Have it with a glass of red and a piece of focaccia to mop up the extra sauce.

serves 3–4

1 onion, diced

2 celery sticks, diced

olive oil, for frying

3 garlic cloves, crushed

2 bay leaves

400g beef mince

½ tbsp dried oregano

500ml passata or ½ quantity of basic
   tomato sauce (see page 244)

1 bunch of basil, leaves only

400g egg lasagne sheets

50g ricotta

FOR THE CHEESE SAUCE

25g butter

25g plain flour

250ml whole milk

170ml double cream

50g Cheddar cheese, plus extra
   for the top

sea salt and white pepper

Dice the onion and celery sticks. Add to a large saucepan with a glug of olive oil and sweat for a few minutes, then add the garlic. Cook for 1 minute, then add the bay leaves and mince and cook for a further 5 minutes. Add the oregano and passata or sauce and cook for 10 minutes to reduce the sauce.

Meanwhile, start the cheese sauce. Melt the butter in a medium saucepan and add the flour. Cook for 1–2 minutes, taking care not to burn. Mix the milk and double cream together in another saucepan and bring up to the boil. Slowly whisk the liquid into the saucepan with the flour mixture. Cook for a few minutes until the sauce thickens, then grate in the Cheddar cheese. Season with salt and white pepper.

Preheat the oven to 200°C (fan 180°C/gas mark 6). Spread a couple of tablespoons of the beef sauce in a medium ovenproof dish and tear over a few basil leaves. Layer the pasta sheets over the mince and cover in a small layer of cheese sauce, then mince, then another layer of pasta, basil and cheese sauce. Repeat until you've used up all of the beef sauce.

Finish with a layer of the cheese sauce. Dot with ricotta and a small grating of Cheddar cheese and bake in the oven for 30 minutes. Serve.

ditalini and
haricot bean

This is vibrant, colourful, delicious and earthy food. It makes me think of a grand Tudor table with a big old pot cooking on the fireplace, with everyone ladling it out in bowls to the family. I love the group vibe of cooking and serving up food. Making food for other people brings me much more happiness than cooking for myself.

serves 4

olive oil, for frying

100g pancetta, diced into
   1cm (½ in) pieces

1 onion, chopped

1 sprig of rosemary

1 sprig of thyme

250g ditalini pasta (or macaroni pasta)

2 garlic cloves, chopped

2 carrots, finely chopped

500ml chicken stock

250g tinned white haricot beans

2 small heads of baby gem lettuce,
   cut into quarters

sea salt and black pepper

100g Fontina cheese, grated or cut into
   1cm (½ in) cubes

crunchy bread, to serve (optional)

Heat a large deep saucepan with a little olive oil and add the diced pancetta. Cook for 5 minutes over a medium heat until golden and crisp and the fat has rendered down. Add the onion, rosemary and thyme and cook for another 5 minutes.

Meanwhile, bring a medium saucepan of water to the boil, and cook the pasta according to packet instructions until al dente.

Add the garlic and carrots to the onion mixture and cook for 2–3 minutes, then add the chicken stock and bring to the boil, then stir through the cooked pasta, haricot beans and baby gem lettuce. Season with salt and pepper and take the pan off the heat.

Stir through the Fontina cheese. Serve with some lightly toasted crunchy bread drizzled with olive oil, if you like.

how to
make pasta

It wasn't until I was eighteen that I started making pasta. I'd been working for Angela Hartnett for three months and I was put on the pasta section. And that was that: I fell in love with using such a simple base ingredient to create a huge range of dishes. People always say to me that making pasta is too hard and time-consuming, needing lots of fancy equipment, but it's actually really easy and cheap. It's my mission to convert people to making pasta.

makes 600g

400g grade Tipo '00' flour
6 medium egg yolks
3 medium eggs
1 tbsp olive oil
semolina flour, for dusting (optional)

SPECIAL EQUIPMENT
pasta machine

Pour the flour into a pile on a clean work surface. Using your fingers, make a well in the top of the pile. Whisk the egg yolks and whole eggs in a bowl, pouring in the olive oil as you go.

Pour the egg mixture into the well in the flour, mixing together with a fork or your fingertips until you reach a light, breadcrumb-like texture. Continue to bring the dough together. Knead for a few minutes to strengthen the gluten – it should become smooth, silky and slightly shiny.

Once you've kneaded the pasta dough, wrap it in cling film and immediately place in the fridge. Leave to rest for at least 30 minutes.

Once the dough has rested, cut it in half and flatten each half with a rolling pin, until you have an almost rectangle shape, the same width as the pasta machine.

Set your pasta machine to its widest setting. Flour your pasta dough and roll it through the machine twice. Then roll the pasta once through each of the settings, working your way down to the second-from-thinnest setting (or the thinnest setting if you want seriously thin pasta).

Cut your pasta into the required shape and either use straightaway, or dust in semolina flour and hang so it dries out. Dried fresh pasta usually keeps for a week or two.

/ If you are short of time, whack the flour into a food processor, pulse while adding the eggs, then knead as above.

MEAT

chapter 5

my chilli

Everyone needs a good chilli recipe and this is my go-to version. Like all good chillies, it's got a real kick, so I serve it with homemade guacamole to add a bit of coolness. I added the crushed tortilla at the end as it gives a nice change in texture. This is perfect for feeding large groups of people and you can also make it in advance and freeze it.

serves 3–4

2 red onions, finely sliced
2 garlic cloves, crushed
olive oil
2 tsp smoked paprika
1 tsp dried coriander
2 tsp ground cumin
1 tsp chilli flakes
2 tbsp brown sugar
500g beef mince
1 × 400g tin of whole tomatoes
400ml hot chicken stock (optional)

FOR THE GUACAMOLE
1 avocado
1 tomato
2 spring onions, finely sliced
1 red chilli, finely sliced
handful of coriander leaves, chopped
juice of 1 lime

TO SERVE
handful of tortilla chips
100g Cheddar cheese, grated

Add the onions, garlic and a glug of olive oil to a large ovenproof frying pan over a medium heat. Fry for a few minutes, then add all the herbs and spices and the sugar and cook for 1 minute. Add the beef mince and cook until it browns.

Add the tomatoes, mushing them down with a fork. Add the boiling chicken stock or 400ml boiling water, then put the lid on and cook for 20 minutes. Remove the lid and cook for another 10 minutes.

While the chilli is cooking, start the guacamole. Simply peel and de-stone the avocado and roughly chop with the tomato. Mix with the sliced spring onions and chilli. Stir through the coriander and lime juice.

When the chilli is cooked, preheat your grill to medium hot. Crush the tortilla chips over the pan and sprinkle with the cheese. Slide the pan underneath the grill for 5 minutes until the cheese is melted. Serve.

gimme the
jerk burger

I love Caribbean food. If I had to choose my 'Death Row dinner' it would definitely be jerk chicken. This is my simple, quick version of a jerk dinner in a burger. You've got the traditional flavours of ginger, garlic and scotch bonnet, and the plantain gives a nice sweetness. The plantain is part of the banana family but it's savoury and goes well with Caribbean food. I could eat ten of these.

serves 2

4 boneless, skinless chicken thighs
olive oil
1 plantain
2 brioche or burger buns
1 head of baby gem lettuce

FOR THE MARINADE
½ scotch bonnet chilli
1 garlic clove
¼ tsp allspice
1 thumbnail of fresh ginger
1 tbsp honey

FOR THE JERK MAYONNAISE
4 tbsp mayonnaise (shop-bought or
  homemade, see page 230)
1 tsp dry jerk seasoning
2 spring onions, thinly sliced
juice of ½ lime

Whack the marinade ingredients into a pestle and mortar, or roughly but finely chop on a board until they become a paste. Spread a glug of olive oil over the chicken thighs, then cover them in the marinade. If you have time, leave the marinade to soak into the chicken for 1 hour, but if not you can cook straightaway.

Preheat the oven to 200°C (fan 180°C/gas mark 6).

Add a glug of oil to a medium ovenproof pan over a medium heat and place the thighs in the pan, skin-side down. Cook for 1 minute on each side, then place the pan in the oven to cook for 7 minutes.

Peel and slice the plantain into thick coins and heat a pan with two big glugs of oil. Add the plantain and cook for 3 minutes on each side, until golden.

While the chicken and plantain are cooking, make the simple jerk mayonnaise by thoroughly mixing all the ingredients in a small bowl.

Slice the buns in half and toast them in a dry frying pan or under a grill.

Dollop the mayo on the top and bottom of the buns, then lay the plantain on the bottom bun. Chop the thighs into strips and place on top of the plantain. Hit with a few lettuce leaves and serve.

aubergine and lamb burgers

Burgers are so versatile and you can do anything with them. This one is a bit different – the aubergine acts like the burger bun, and because aubergine has that nice meatiness to it, you still feel like you've got a substantial burger. It makes a nice change to a regular burger if you don't want to have bread or want to go low-carb.

serves 2

500g lamb mince
1 onion, chopped
3 garlic cloves, crushed
1 heaped tsp chilli flakes
1 heaped tsp ground cumin
large handful of parsley, chopped
1 large aubergine
olive oil, for drizzling
sea salt and black pepper
flat breads, to serve
few dollops of hummus, to serve

FOR THE MINTED YOGHURT
1 bunch of mint, leaves finely
  chopped into a paste
300ml Greek yoghurt
juice of ½ lemon

Start by firing up the grill to get it ready for the lamb burgers and aubergine.

Place the lamb mince, onion and garlic in a large bowl. Add the chilli flakes, cumin and chopped parsley. Mix it all together with your hands, being sure to bind all the ingredients nicely. Form the lamb into two extra-large burgers and leave in the fridge while you prepare the aubergine.

Slice the aubergine into four 2.5cm (1in) slices, drizzle with olive oil and season with salt and pepper. Pop the lamb burgers and the aubergine on a baking sheet. Place under the hot grill for 2 minutes on each side, then remove the burgers from the grill and leave to rest, leaving the aubergine slices to grill for another minute on each side.

Meanwhile, make a quick and easy minted yoghurt. Mix together the mint, Greek yoghurt and a large pinch of salt. Squeeze in the lemon juice and give it all a good stir.

Take two pieces of aubergine and use them to sandwich one of the lamb burgers. Repeat with the other aubergine slices and lamb burger and serve with a dollop of the minted yoghurt on top. Pile the flat breads and hummus on the side of the plates and serve.

/ If you're feeling a little more adventurous, you could always make your own hummus!

pork chops and
roasted cauliflower

Pork chops are seen as very old school and retro now – they were the kind of thing you used to have as a kid on a Sunday, along with applesauce. You don't really see them much on restaurant menus but I want to bring them back. This is another classic with a twist: I've roasted the cauli because it's always good to ramp up your veggies!

serves 2

1 tbsp olive oil, plus extra for oiling
  and frying
1 head of cauliflower
1 tsp ground turmeric
sea salt and black pepper
2 pork chops
2½ tbsp classic vinaigrette
  (see page 236)
50g sultanas
100g watercress

Preheat the oven to 180°C (fan 160°C/gas mark 4).

Oil a baking tray and line it with greaseproof paper. Break or cut the cauliflower head into florets, then toss in 1 tablespoon olive oil, the turmeric and a pinch of salt. Roast in the oven for 20–25 minutes.

While the cauliflower is roasting, wrap the pork chops in cling film and bash with a rolling pin. This helps the meat to cook more quickly. Season the pork with a glug of olive oil, salt and pepper.

Add another glug of olive oil to a medium frying pan over a medium heat and fry the chops for about 4 minutes on each side, or until cooked the whole way through.

Remove the cauliflower from the oven and toss in a bowl with 2 tablespoons of the vinaigrette and the sultanas. Dress the watercress with the remaining vinaigrette, and serve.

lamb jalapeño pittas

I love kebabs. People think they're naughty and something you only eat when you're starving after a night out, but when you make them at home, they're actually healthy and tick all the boxes: meat, bread and salad in one. This is my version of a doner. Make sure you use good-quality lamb mince with high fat content so the koftas don't dry out.

serves 4

400g lamb mince
1 tsp ground cumin
1 tsp smoked paprika
1 tsp cayenne pepper
1 tsp fennel seeds
1 garlic clove, crushed
100g feta cheese
olive oil, for frying
4 pittas
Greek yoghurt, to serve (optional)

FOR THE JALAPEÑO SALSA
6 green jalapeños
1 small bunch of coriander
2 tbsp white wine vinegar
100ml olive oil
sea salt and black pepper

Preheat the oven to 200°C (fan 180°C/gas mark 6).

To make the koftas, mix the lamb mince in a bowl with all the spices and garlic and bind together with your hands. Form into sixteen slightly flattened balls. Pop a small thumb-sized piece of feta cheese in the middle of each one.

Place a glug of olive oil in a large ovenproof pan over a medium heat and fry your koftas for a few minutes on each side until dark and golden, then transfer the pan to the oven and cook for a further 7 minutes.

While the koftas are cooking, make the salsa. Finely chop the jalapeños and the coriander and mix together in a medium bowl with the vinegar and olive oil. Season with salt and pepper.

Toast the pittas and slice them open at the top. Fill with three or four koftas and drizzle with jalapeño salsa. If you'd like to cool the pittas down, add a dollop of Greek yoghurt.

salt beef with potato latkes

This is inspired by all the salt-beef bagels I've eaten on Brick Lane in East London. I wanted to change it up a bit so I added the potato. Like my steak, eggs and salsa verde (see page 133) this is a versatile dish you can eat at any time, as a more substantial breakfast, or else for lunch or dinner. I am a fiend for American mustard; the more mustard on this one the better!

serves 2–3

2 large Maris Piper potatoes
1 medium egg yolk
white pepper
1 tbsp plain flour
1 onion, roughly chopped
olive oil
sea salt
200g salt beef slices
2 whole pickles, sliced thinly
yellow mustard, to serve

Peel the potatoes and grate them into a bowl. Rinse the potato under cold water and pop into a colander to drain off all the water. Place them back into a bowl and mix through the egg yolk, a pinch of white pepper and the flour.

Add the onion and a glug of oil to a medium saucepan over a low heat. Cover and sweat until it is caramelized and golden – about 8–10 minutes. Remove the pan from the heat and add the potato mixture. Combine everything together, adding a pinch of salt. Form into 4–6 rough pancake-like discs.

Add a big glug of olive oil to a large frying pan over a medium heat. Add the potato latkes and fry gently for a few minutes on each side, until golden. Try not to move them around the pan as they might stick.

Remove the latkes from the pan and place straight onto a piece of kitchen roll.

Add the salt beef into the pan you used for the cakes, just to heat it through.

Lay the cakes on a plate and tear over the salt beef. Top with thin strips of pickle and drizzle with the yellow mustard.

bake-me-up meatballs

This is a delicious, classic Italian dish. It's so rich and hearty and easy to put together, you can make it for two or ten people. It's very *The Godfather* – you can just picture all the gangsters sitting around the table eating meatballs. Baking the meatballs gives a deeper, darker structure to the flavour, and I've added my beloved burrata for extra-special ooziness. You can serve with spaghetti or some bread to mop up the sauce.

250g beef mince
250g veal mince
1 medium egg
50g breadcrumbs
160g Parmesan, grated
1 small bunch of parsley, chopped
few sprigs of fresh oregano, chopped
1 large onion, finely chopped
3 garlic cloves, crushed
1 quantity of basic tomato sauce
   (see page 244), or 1 litre passata
olive oil
1 ball of burrata
sourdough bread or spaghetti, to serve

Mix the beef and veal mince in a large bowl with the egg, breadcrumbs, half the Parmesan, parsley, oregano, onion and garlic. Mix all the ingredients together to form 12–16 equal-sized balls.

Make the tomato sauce, if using (see page 244).

Preheat the oven to 200°C (fan 180°C/gas mark 6).

Warm a few glugs of olive oil in a large ovenproof frying pan over a medium heat. Fry the meatballs for a few minutes on each side, until golden and caramelized.

Once you've coloured the meatballs, pour over the tomato sauce or passata and pop in the oven for 30 minutes.

Remove the pan from the oven and tear and dot the burrata in and around the meatballs. Grate the remaining Parmesan over the top and pop back in the oven for another 5 minutes, so the cheese melts to become gorgeous and gooey.

Eat with slabs of sourdough bread or serve with freshly cooked spaghetti.

steak, eggs
and salsa verde

This is a great lunch or dinner, but it would make a good breakfast after you've hit the gym as it's very protein heavy, but still healthy. It's made of only three components, but it looks and tastes fantastic. If you can, always shop organic or free range for your eggs and meat. Get your steak from your local butcher if you can spend that little bit more. I always go to the market to get my herbs – they're cheaper and more flavoursome. For me, it's always about quality over quantity.

serves 2

1 quantity of salsa verde (see page 240)
2 thick sirloin steaks
olive oil
sea salt and black pepper
1 tsp white wine vinegar
2 medium eggs

Start by making the salsa verde (see page 240). Add more olive oil if necessary – the looser the salsa verde the better, as you'll be drizzling it over the steak and eggs.

Heat a griddle pan to searing hot, and bring a small pan of water to the boil for the poached eggs.

Drizzle the steaks with olive oil, and season with salt and pepper. Place the steaks on the griddle pan and cook for 2 minutes on each side, until medium rare. Transfer the steaks to a cooling rack over the pan and leave to rest for 4 minutes.

Meanwhile, drop the white wine vinegar into the boiling water and crack the eggs in gently. Poach the eggs for a couple of minutes and when cooked, use a slotted spoon to carefully transfer to a piece of kitchen roll.

Pop an egg on top of each rested steak and drizzle with salsa verde.

/ You can make the salsa verde ahead of time and keep it in the fridge for up to a week. It also tastes amazing with mashed potato!

duck and orange coleslaw wraps

This is basically Peking Duck in a wrap – and it's delicious! Orange is a very traditional flavour for pairing with strong-flavoured duck, but I added the beetroot for that nice bit of extra earthiness. It is quite easy to overcook duck – I think people avoid cooking with it as a result – but if you take your time and give it care it's simple to get right.

serves 4

2 duck breasts
sea salt
1 tsp five spice
4 tortilla wraps

FOR THE SLAW
1 carrot
1 small kohlrabi
1 small beetroot
1 orange
1 red onion, finely sliced
1 celery stick, finely sliced
100g Greek yoghurt

Preheat the oven to 200°C (fan 180°C/gas mark 6).

Rub the skin-side of the duck breasts with a healthy pinch of salt and the five spice. Add the duck, skin-side down, to a cold large ovenproof pan and slowly bring up to a medium to high heat. This method renders the fat and gives you a crispy skin. Cook for about 6 minutes until the skin is golden, then flip over and brown the other side for 1 minute. Slide the pan into the oven to cook for a further 8 minutes.

Once the meat is cooked – you want it nice and pink in the centre – leave it to rest for 10 minutes. Meanwhile, make the slaw.

Peel the carrot, kohlrabi and beetroot and top and tail them. Grate or thinly slice into strips, then transfer to a medium bowl.

Grate the zest of the orange into the veg bowl. Remove the orange pith and slice the segments into the bowl, along with the onion and celery. Mix everything together along with a pinch of salt and the Greek yoghurt.

Slice the rested duck breasts, and place on a large serving plate alongside the bowl of slaw. Heat up the wraps and build your own.

rump steak baguettes
with chimichurri

When I was in my early twenties I was lucky enough to live in Buenos Aires for three months and I had the best time. Argentinean meat is amazing and it gets cooked on 'asados', which are kind of like barbecues. It's seen as a real privilege to cook on an asado – the father teaches the son and so on. Everyone sits around the table to eat and share. It's got a community, family feel, which I love. I adore chimichurri, it's so flavoursome that you don't need much else with it.

serves 2

500g rump steak
olive oil
sea salt and black pepper
2 small baguettes
100g Manchego cheese

FOR THE CHIMICHURRI
1 red chilli
3 garlic cloves, crushed
2 tbsp red wine vinegar
100ml olive oil
80g bunch of parsley

Heat a griddle pan to searing hot. Drizzle the steak in olive oil, season with salt and pepper and whack it on the griddle pan. Sear each side for 2 minutes, until medium rare. Remove it from the heat and leave to rest for at least 4 minutes.

While the steak is resting, make the chimichurri. Finely chop the chilli and add to a small bowl, along with the finely crushed garlic, a pinch of salt and pepper, the red wine vinegar and olive oil. Pick and roughly chop the parsley leaves and add to the bowl. Mix it all together.

Slice the baguettes down the middle and place on the griddle pan for 1 minute to warm up. Slice the rump steak and divide between the two baguettes. Drizzle with loads of chimichurri and shavings of the Manchego, and serve.

*Often cheaper
than sirloin,
rump steak
tastes incredible*

peanut chicken thighs
and ribbon veg

Lots of people prefer almond or cashew butter these days, but peanut butter is still a healthy option and has a lot going for it. It also works really well with chicken. This is a spicier version of a normal satay sauce. The red curry sauce is quite intense and rich so I've kept it light with ribbon veg, which brings freshness.

serves 2

4 boneless, skinless chicken thighs
olive oil
pinch of sea salt
1 thumbnail of fresh ginger, grated

FOR THE SATAY SAUCE
1 tsp coconut oil
1 shallot, finely chopped
1 garlic clove, crushed
1 tbsp red curry paste
4 tbsp crunchy peanut butter
200ml coconut milk
zest and juice of 1 lime

FOR THE RIBBON VEG
1 carrot, peeled into strips using
   a peeler
1 cucumber, peeled into strips using
   a peeler
1 Granny Smith apple, peeled and
   cut into thin strips
½ white cabbage, cored and
   finely sliced
1 red onion, sliced
25g coriander, chopped, plus
   extra sprigs for serving

Place each chicken thigh between two pieces of greaseproof paper and bash it with a rolling pin to make it a little thinner. Drizzle olive oil over the thighs and top with the salt and grated ginger. Rub all over the chicken.

Heat a griddle pan to searing hot. Add the chicken and cook for a few minutes on each side, until lightly charred and fully cooked. Transfer the chicken to a piece of kitchen roll to rest.

Meanwhile, start the satay sauce. Melt the coconut oil in a medium saucepan over a low to medium heat and add the shallot and garlic. Fry for a few minutes, then add the red curry paste and cook for another minute. Add the peanut butter and coconut milk. Stirring continuously, bring to the boil, then add the lime zest and juice and remove from the heat. Set aside.

Put all the ribbon veg ingredients in a large bowl, then add a pinch of salt and stir in most of the satay sauce, saving some to drizzle over the chicken.

Cut the chicken into wide strips. Divide the ribbon veg between two bowls, then top with the chicken and the reserved satay sauce.

harissa chicken legs with quinoa and avocado

This is a Moroccan-inspired dish. It's a great little number for the family – chicken legs are quite cheap so this is good for anyone who's cooking on a budget. Chicken legs are also really easy to cook and make a nice change from a fillet. You get the good fats from the avocados and quinoa is a great source of fibre.

serves 4

95g rose harissa
olive oil
sea salt and black pepper
1 red onion, quartered
4 skin-on chicken legs
300g quinoa
1 garlic clove, crushed
2 avocados
juice of ½ lemon

Preheat the oven to 200°C (fan 180°C/gas mark 6).

In a bowl combine the harissa, a glug of olive oil and salt. Add the red onion to the bowl, then add the chicken and mix together, making sure everything is evenly coated. Lay it all out on a roasting tray and roast in the oven for 35–40 minutes until the chicken is cooked through.

Heat a medium saucepan and add the dry quinoa. Toast for 1 minute, then add the garlic and 800ml cold water. Cover with a lid and bring up to the boil, adding a pinch of salt and pepper. Cook for about 15 minutes until nearly all the liquid has gone.

Meanwhile peel and de-stone the avocados. Dice them roughly and squeeze over the lemon juice. Sprinkle with another pinch of salt.

Divide the quinoa and chicken between four plates and serve with the avocado.

FISH

chapter 6

pan-seared scallops and lentils

I love scallops – they're so sweet and delicious. You see them a lot on menus in restaurants, but it's rare for people to try them at home, even though they are so easy to cook. I'm using pre-cooked lentils here, so you can make an amazing dinner in less than 10 minutes. This dish is great for getting in the carbs and protein.

serves 2

10–12 scallops (120–150g per person)
sea salt and black pepper
olive oil
250g pre-cooked Puy lentils
handful of chives, chopped
200g spinach
1 garlic clove, crushed

Warm a plate in a low oven. Season the scallops with salt and a few cracks of pepper. Warm a glug of olive oil in a large non-stick frying pan on a very high heat.

Gradually add the scallops into the pan, starting at the 12 o'clock position at the top of the pan and working your way round until the last one is in. Cook for about 1 minute until the underside is golden, then turn them over, starting from the 12 o'clock position. When golden on both sides, transfer the scallops onto the warmed plate, again starting from the 12 o'clock position.

Pop the lentils into the same pan with a splash of olive oil, then season and reheat for a minute until piping hot. Arrange the lentils on two plates, place the scallops on top and garnish with chives.

Quickly wilt the spinach in the scorching hot pan with the crushed garlic, a splash of olive oil and a pinch of salt. Serve alongside.

haddock and parsley mash

This is such an English dish. Haddock is one of the meatier fishes, so I think this is like the fish version of sausage and mash or steak and mash. The earthiness of the potato and parsley go well together. I eat this with a nice glass of red. People always think white wine and fish go together, but that's not always true – a glass of red goes really well with a meaty fish.

serves 2

500g Maris Piper potatoes, peeled and cut in half
sea salt
100ml whole milk
60g butter
white pepper
1 bunch of parsley, leaves picked
olive oil, for frying
2 × 150g skin-on haddock fillets

Place the potatoes in a pan of salted cold water and bring up to the boil. Once they've reached boiling, turn the heat down to a simmer for about 20 minutes, or until soft and cooked in the centre. You can easily check with the tip of a knife.

Place the milk, butter and a pinch of salt and white pepper in a small saucepan over a medium heat and bring up to the boil. Set aside. (This is the emulsion for the mash once the potatoes are cooked.)

Just before the potatoes are ready, add the parsley leaves to the saucepan to blanch them for 30 seconds. Drain the potatoes and mash the parsley and potatoes together using a masher or ricer.

Place the mash back into the pan and add the butter and milk emulsion, stirring until combined.

Heat a frying pan with a glug of olive oil. Season the fish fillets and fry skin-side down for 3 minutes, then flip and lightly cook the other side for a minute or until just cooked.

Plate with the mashed potato and serve.

poached salmon
niçoise

I love creating new dishes, but I also love my classics. This salad is normally made with pan-seared tuna, but I added the salmon for a different twist. It's light, fresh and just lovely: another great summer dish. Some people get 'weirded out' by fusion cooking and some stuff is too gimmicky (for instance, I'm not a fan of Indian tacos), but there are some things you can mix and match, and this is one of them.

serves 2

240g green beans
2 × 120g salmon fillets
2 large eggs

FOR THE ANCHOVY DRESSING
3 anchovies
1 tsp olive oil
3 tbsp crème fraîche
juice of ½ lemon
black pepper

TO SERVE
6 black olives, pitted
handful of chives, chopped

Bring a medium saucepan or steamer pan of salted boiling water to the boil. Add the green beans to the water and cover with a colander or steamer inset. Put the salmon fillets inside the colander or steamer inset, then cover with a lid and cook the green beans and salmon for 6–8 minutes, taking the green beans out a couple of minutes earlier so that they still hold a slight crunch.

Bring a small saucepan of water to the boil. Drop the eggs in gently, trying not to crack them. Boil for 5–6 minutes so you still have a slightly runny but set yolk.

To make the dressing, bash the anchovies to a paste in a small bowl with the olive oil. Add the crème fraîche, lemon juice and a crack of pepper. (You don't need to season with salt, as the anchovies are salty enough.)

Flake the cooked salmon with a fork and peel the eggs under cold running water. Chop each egg into quarters.

Stir half the dressing through the green beans and transfer onto two plates, dotting the egg, flaked salmon and olives in and around the green beans. Sprinkle with chives and drizzle the rest of the dressing around the plate.

octopus and chorizo stew

This is my take on a classic one-pot Spanish dish, which is great if you're cooking for a crowd. You get so much flavour from the chorizo and all the lovely herbs. There are a number of seafood ingredients that I think people are scared to cook, and octopus is one of them. It's actually really easy and a lot of supermarkets sell them already cleaned, or you could buy from a fishmonger and they'll do it for you. Focaccia is perfect for mopping up all the leftover juices.

serves 4

100g chorizo
olive oil
16 baby octopus, cleaned
12 new potatoes, cut into quarters
2 garlic cloves, crushed
3 anchovies
1 tbsp capers
225g cherry tomatoes
small handful of black olives, pitted
1 red chilli, deseeded and sliced
150–200ml dry white wine
25g bunch of parsley, chopped
splash of sherry vinegar
focaccia, cornbread or polenta,
  to serve

Chop the chorizo into coins. Heat a large lidded saucepan with a couple of glugs of olive oil. Add the chorizo and cook for 1 minute, then transfer to a plate, keeping the chorizo oil in the pan.

Add the baby octopus and the quartered potatoes and fry for 1 minute over a medium heat. Add the garlic, anchovies, capers, cherry tomatoes, black olives and chilli. Fry for 1 minute, then add the white wine and 150ml water. Add the chorizo back in, cover and cook for 30 minutes. (You don't need to season with salt, as the anchovies and capers are salty enough.)

Add the parsley to the pan, along with a glug of olive oil and the sherry vinegar. Serve in bowls with focaccia, cornbread or polenta.

herby prawn
burger with
lime mayo

Did I mention that I love burgers? You rarely see prawn burgers on menus but they make a great alternative to the classics. You simply mince the raw prawns by hand, then add the herbs. You've got loads of flavours in there, plus the richness of the prawns – then the lime comes through and smacks you in the face. This is another fresh and zingy one: think Mexico meets Japan meets a good old American-style burger.

serves 2

2 spring onions, finely sliced
½ bunch of coriander, leaves
  chopped
240g raw king prawns
sea salt
olive oil
100g mayonnaise (shop-bought
  or see page 230)
zest of 1 lime and juice of ½ lime
2 brioche buns
100g rocket
1 red chilli, deseeded and sliced

Mix the spring onions with the coriander. Add the raw king prawns to the herb mix and transfer to a chopping board.

Roughly chop the prawns with the herb mix until you get a fine mince-like paste. Season with salt, cover and chill in the fridge for at least 30 minutes.

Divide the chilled mixture into two equal parts. Cover your hands in olive oil and shape two burger patties.

Heat a glug of oil in a large non-stick pan over a medium to high heat. Add the burgers and cook for 2–3 minutes each side, until golden but slightly pink.

In a small bowl, mix the mayonnaise with the lime zest and juice. Add a pinch of salt and mix.

Remove the patties from the heat. Slice the buns in half and toast until golden.

Cover both sides of the brioche buns with a healthy dollop of the mayo. Sandwich the burgers in the buns topped with a handful of rocket and the chilli.

/ Leave any leftover mayo covered in the fridge. It will last about a week and it's always handy to have a bit of extra in the house!

mackerel with samphire and new potatoes

Salty samphire is now pretty easy to find in supermarkets when in season. We also have great English mackerel, which I love to cook. I always try to buy seasonal produce: it's better quality, reduces the carbon footprint and supports our own home-grown economy. Mackerel is great for essential healthy oils and you can make this dish even simpler by using leftover potatoes.

serves 2

2 mackerel fillets
olive oil
sea salt and black pepper
pinch of cayenne pepper
6 new potatoes
100g samphire
knob of butter
2 garlic cloves, crushed
½ tsp chilli flakes
classic vinaigrette, to serve
  (see page 236)

Preheat the oven to 200°C (fan 180°C/gas mark 6) and line a baking tray with greaseproof paper.

Lay the fish on the tray and drizzle with a glug of olive oil, a pinch of salt and pepper and the cayenne pepper. Bake the fish for 8–10 minutes until cooked through nicely.

Meanwhile, place the new potatoes in a pan of cold water and boil for 15 minutes until soft in the centre. Remove the potatoes with a slotted spoon, reserving the water in the pan. Bring the water back to the boil and blanch the samphire for 2 minutes.

Slice the potatoes into round slices and pop into a large frying pan, with a glug of olive oil and the butter. Fry until lightly golden brown, then add the garlic, chilli flakes and samphire. Cook all together for 2 minutes, before serving with the fish and the classic vinaigrette.

sea bass with apple and celeriac slaw

I don't love celeriac when it's cooked but I really like it raw. It has quite a strong aniseed taste, but also has apple-like flavour, so it complements the other ingredients in this recipe. Sea bass is probably one of the best fish out there. I don't normally eat the skin on fish (for instance I don't eat salmon skin), but on sea bass the skin is thinner and really crisp and flavoursome when cooked like this. Delicious.

serves 2

2 × 300g whole sea bass, gutted
  and scaled
olive oil
1 tsp cayenne pepper
sea salt and black pepper
2 tbsp goji berries, to serve

FOR THE SLAW
1 small head of celeriac
1 apple (Granny Smith)
zest and juice of 1 lemon

Score the sea bass skin with a small knife, leaving a thumb-size gap between each score. Drizzle in olive oil and sprinkle with the cayenne pepper, salt and pepper.

To make the slaw, peel the celeriac and grate it into a bowl along with the apple. Add a pinch of salt and the lemon zest and juice.

Whack a large non-stick frying pan over a medium to high heat. Add a glug of olive oil and lay the seasoned sea bass in the pan. Cook for 3–5 minutes on each side, until golden crisp and cooked through nicely.

Plate with the slaw and a sprinkling of goji berries.

/ The lemon juice stops the celeriac and apple from oxidizing and turning brown, and also gives a fresh flavour.

monkfish
red curry

Like scallops, monkfish is really underused. I love that monkfish has a really meaty, firm texture – you can whack it into soups and curries and it won't go flaky and disintegrate, but still holds its shape. This is an easy one to make when you have mates round – serve up and eat it in front of the telly.

serves 2–4

nut or vegetable oil
500g monkfish, chopped into 4–6cm
  (2½–3½ in) pieces
1 heaped tbsp red curry paste
1 kaffir lime leaf
1 × 400ml tin of coconut milk
2 heads of pak choi
1 red chilli, chopped finely
handful of fresh coriander
cooked rice, to serve (optional)

Heat a glug of oil in a large saucepan over a medium heat. Add the monkfish to the pan along with the red curry paste and lime leaf and cook and stir for 1 minute. Add the coconut milk and bring to the boil, then return to a simmer.

Cut the pak choi into quarters, then add to the curry and cook for 2 minutes.

Serve in a bowl and dress with chopped chilli and coriander. Serve on its own or with a side of cooked rice.

crab pie

I ate my first ever pie as a kid when I went with my dad to watch Tottenham Hotspurs play. I had a chicken and mushroom one with chips and I've loved pies ever since. This crab pie is a more elegant version – you probably wouldn't eat this on the terrace, but it would go down very well at a dinner party! It's also definitely more refined to serve it with salad instead of chips.

serves 4

300–400g Maris Piper potatoes (about 3), peeled
knob of butter
sea salt and black pepper
pinch of white pepper
1 sprig of thyme, leaves only
60g Cheddar cheese, grated
fresh mixed salad, to serve (optional)

FOR THE CRAB FILLING
olive oil, for frying
1 onion, diced
2 garlic cloves, crushed
150ml double cream
300g crab meat (mix of 50/50 white and brown meat)
150g spinach leaves

Chop the potatoes into equal-sized chunks and place in a saucepan of cold salted water. Bring to the boil and cook for 15–20 minutes, or until the potato softens and becomes crumbly. Drain thoroughly.

Add the butter, a pinch of salt, the white pepper, thyme leaves and half of the cheese to the saucepan. Mash it all together roughly.

Preheat the oven to 200°C (fan 180°C/gas mark 6).

For the crab filling, heat a glug of olive oil in a medium-sized pan over a medium heat, then add the onion and garlic, cover and sweat for 6–8 minutes until pale and translucent.

Add the cream and crab meat. Bring the cream up to the boil, then simmer for a few minutes until the cream thickens. Add the spinach and remove from the heat. Season with salt and pepper.

Transfer the crab filling to a heatproof dish. Spoon the mash over the top of the crab sauce and add the rest of the cheese. Pop in the oven for 15 minutes, or until the top turns a gorgeous golden brown colour.

Serve on its own or with a fresh mixed salad.

tuna tartare
with sorrel

I've eaten some great tuna tartare in my time. I've had it at fancy places like Nobu, I've had a ceviche version in Mexico and an incredible one in Japan. So this is my version of all the great ones I've tasted around the world. With this dish, always go for good-quality tuna. Either go to your local fishmongers or fish counter, or use sushi-grade tuna. Don't just go to the supermarket and get a tuna steak.

serves 2

1 × 300g fresh tuna loin
ice cubes
1 tbsp English runny honey
1 garlic clove, crushed
zest and juice of 1 lemon
sea salt and black pepper
2 tbsp olive oil, plus extra for drizzling
12 chives, chopped
2 thick slices of sourdough bread
30g sorrel, preferably micro

Start by finely dicing the tuna into 1cm (½in) cubes, discarding any dark, bloody or sinewy flesh. Pop straight into a bowl over ice and place in the fridge while you make the dressing.

Mix the honey, garlic, lemon zest and juice in a bowl, with a pinch of salt, the olive oil and half the chives. Check the seasoning – you want it to be slightly overly salty.

Drizzle both sides of the sourdough bread in olive oil and toast in a dry pan or under the grill.

Meanwhile, mix the tuna into the dressing. The tuna will turn a slight pale white colour – that's the lemon 'cooking' the tuna.

Mix a little dressing with the sorrel. Load it all on top of the warm toasted sourdough and serve, garnished with the remaining chives.

VEGAN

chapter 7

courgette and farro salad

Farro is a such an old wheat, and even the name sounds whimsical and poetic. It's an underused grain that's delicious, chewy and wholesome with a really nutty taste. This is a great little number – you've got the smokiness from the grilled pepper, then the lemon dressing zings it up a bit and opens your palate.

serves 2–3

200g farro
2 courgettes, cut into 2cm (¾ in) coins
2 tbsp olive oil
sea salt and black pepper
200g jarred whole piquillo peppers,
    drained and roughly chopped
1 red onion, sliced
25g mint, leaves only

TO SERVE
drizzle of soya yoghurt or classic
    vinaigrette (see page 236)
zest of ½ lemon

At least 30 minutes before cooking, soak the farro.

Meanwhile, place the courgettes in a medium bowl with the olive oil and a pinch of salt and pepper. Transfer the slices to a hot griddle pan and cook for about 6 minutes on each side until you get the tasty smoked charred lines. Place the charred courgette back in the bowl and stir through the peppers, red onion and mint leaves.

Drain the farro and cover with cold water. Bring up to the boil, then down to a simmer for 25–30 minutes. One minute before the end of cooking, season with salt.

Drain the farro and add to the bowl of veg. Mix through. Dress with soya yoghurt or classic vinaigrette and top with the lemon zest just before serving.

chickpea pancakes
and wilted greens

This reminds me of my first trip to Dubai. There is a big Indian food scene over there and these pancakes are similar to an Indian dosa. I like the fresh flavour along with mellow Indian spice. If you want to change these from vegan you can add a bit of cheese – maybe some Manchego or another nutty variety.

serves 2

150g chickpea flour
sea salt and black pepper
¼ tsp ground cumin
¼ tsp fennel seeds
¼ tsp ground coriander
olive oil

FOR THE FILLING
200g rainbow chard, roughly chopped
juice of ½ lemon
50g tinned sweetcorn, drained
1 avocado, de-stoned and sliced

TO SERVE
dollop of soya yoghurt
drizzle of chilli oil (see page 234)
50g sunflower seeds

Mix the chickpea flour in a bowl with a pinch of salt and all the spices. Whisk to combine, then pour 200ml tepid water into the bowl, whisking continuously to make a thin pancake batter. Set aside.

To make the filling, add the chard and a little oil to a medium frying pan over a medium heat. Add a pinch of salt and cook until the chard has wilted. Just before you take it out of the pan, add the lemon juice and sweetcorn.

Heat a glug of olive oil in a frying pan and and pour in a ladle of the batter. Cook the batter for a few minutes on each side until golden, then remove from the heat and transfer to a warm oven. Repeat until you have used up all the batter.

Lay the pancakes on a plate and fill them with the chard mixture and slices of avocado. Drizzle with the soya yoghurt and chilli oil and sprinkle with the sunflower seeds.

udon and spiced agave veg

There is a vegan restaurant in London called CookDaily and I'm obsessed with one of the noodle bowls on the menu. It's spicy and sweet with tons of good veggies and noodles. Udon noodles are one of my favourite type of noodles because they're nice and thick with a great bite to them. This is my take on chef King Cook's dish.

serves 4

sea salt
250g udon noodles
olive oil
1 head of broccoli, cut into florets
1 courgette, cut into 1cm (¾ in)
  half moons
6 spring onions, sliced
1 onion, quartered
160g baby sugarsnap peas
150g beansprouts

FOR THE TOPPING
15g coriander
80g peanuts
zest of 1 lime

FOR THE SAUCE
60g agave nectar or rice syrup
30g Sriracha sauce
juice of 1 lime
1 tbsp light soy sauce

To make the topping, chop the coriander and peanuts together either by hand or in a food processor. Mix through the lime zest and set aside.

Make the sauce by simply mixing all the ingredients together in a small bowl. Set aside.

Bring a large pan of salted water to the boil. Add the udon noodles and cook for about 7 minutes or according to packet instructions.

A couple of minutes before the noodles are ready, hit a large pan or wok with a glug of oil. Add all the veg and stir-fry over a medium heat for a few minutes, then add the sauce. Cook for 1 minute and then stir through the cooked noodles.

Divide into four bowls and crumble the topping over each bowl.

miso soup with Sriracha-roasted sweet potato

The heavyweight of hot sauces, Sriracha is a popular sauce from Asia with a massive punch of flavours in the mouth: sweet, salty, sugary and spicy. Miso is a great base for vegan soups and dishes and I've added the sweet potatoes to give it all a bit more chunk.

serves 2

1 sweet potato, peeled and chopped into 2cm (¾ in) dice
1 tbsp sesame oil
2 tbsp Sriracha
4 tbsp miso paste
800ml kombu dashi stock
½ white cabbage, finely chopped
100g silken tofu
½ red chilli, finely sliced

Line a baking tray with greaseproof paper and preheat the oven to 200°C (fan 180°C/gas mark 6).

Mix the sweet potato in a bowl with the sesame oil, the Sriracha and 2 tablespoons of the miso paste. Massage the sauce into the sweet potato, then transfer to the lined tray and roast for 25 minutes.

Meanwhile, bring the dashi stock up to the boil in a medium pan. Add the cabbage and cook for 2 minutes, then take the stock off the boil and stir in the remaining miso paste and the tofu.

Divide the sweet potato between two bowls and ladle in the miso soup. Finish with a few slices of chopped chilli.

rainbow tomato
and bean salad
with basil pesto

This salad is basically a rainbow on a plate. You get loads of protein from the beans, so it's so filling you don't need to serve it with anything else. The watercress gives you a nice hit of pepper and the pesto adds another fresh flavour. It's great in summertime as it has an 'in your garden with a glass of white wine' kind of vibe.

serves 6

660g haricot beans (I like the jars that come in this quantity, but tins will work)
zest and juice of 1 lemon
100ml olive oil, plus extra for drizzling
sea salt
200g mixed rainbow tomatoes, halved
30g pine nuts
30g vegan hard cheese, grated
1 garlic clove, crushed
25g basil, roughly torn
1 tbsp nutritional yeast (optional)
100g watercress

Drain and rinse the beans. Pop them in a bowl and mix with the zest and half the lemon juice. Drizzle with a little olive oil and add a pinch of salt. Mix in the tomatoes and leave the whole thing to marinate while you make the pesto.

Toast the pine nuts in a dry frying pan for 1–2 minutes. Allow to cool, then add them to a food processor or pestle and mortar with the vegan hard cheese, remaining lemon juice, garlic, basil and 100ml olive oil. Blend into a smooth paste, then add the nutritional yeast, if using. If you want a runnier pesto, add more olive oil.

Hit a large plate with the pesto and spread it around. Layer on the beans and tomatoes and top with the watercress and a few dollops of pesto here and there.

/ If you want an authentic cheesy flavour, add the nutritional yeast, although this recipe is also delicious with vegan cheese.

cauliflower cakes

This is a twist on a potato rosti I used to make when I was a Saturday boy for my dad in the restaurant. One of my jobs was grating about a million potatoes to make crispy potato rostis. The amount of time and finesse it took to get the rostis perfectly crisp and brown on either side ... I have never concentrated on something so much in my life! Having said that, these are really simple to cook. Just watch out for the water content in the cauliflower mixture before you start frying because you don't want it to be too soggy.

sea salt

1 × 500g head of cauliflower, cored and cut into florets

olive oil, for frying

1 onion, diced

1 garlic clove, crushed

1 tsp smoked paprika

40g strong flour

50g vegan hard cheese, grated

15g chives, chopped

pinch of smoked sea salt (optional)

TO SERVE

green salad

dollop of dirty chilli sauce (see page 243)

Bring a pan of salted water to the boil over a medium heat. Add the cauliflower and boil for 3 minutes. Drain, then set aside to stand for 5 minutes.

Meanwhile, hit a saucepan with a small amount of olive oil and sweat the onion for 2 minutes. Add the garlic and smoked paprika and sweat for another 3 minutes.

Add the cauliflower to the onion and stir in the flour. Cook for 1 minute.

Either transfer the mixture to a food processor and pulse for 10 seconds, or chop the mixture until fine on a chopping board. Allow the mixture to cool, then add the vegan hard cheese, chives and a pinch of smoked sea salt, if using.

Form the cauliflower into 6–8 cakes. Either fry them in a splash of oil for 3 minutes on each side and serve straightaway, or make the cakes in advance and allow them to firm up in the fridge for an hour before frying.

Serve with a simple salad and the dirty sauce.

/ Boiling the cauliflower partly cooks it, takes some of the bitterness away and makes it easier to form into cakes.

dirty mushroom
nut roast

This is one of my favourite vegan recipes: a quick, deconstructed version of nut roast. I cook it for my family, because my sister and mum are both vegetarian. I think nut roasts get a bad rap because they can either be too dry or too soggy. With this one, I've broken down the elements so it's easier and it looks way more elegant. The cranberries give it an extra fruity punch.

serves 2

400g wild mushrooms

50g pine nuts

50g cashews

10g sunflower seeds

½ tsp fennel seeds

1 onion, thinly sliced

100g vegan butter or margarine,
  plus extra for frying

2 garlic cloves, crushed

100g vegan breadcrumbs

1 sprig of rosemary, leaves picked

sea salt and black pepper

6–8 fennel fronds, plus extra
  for serving

30g cranberries

½ bunch of parsley, roughly chopped

Clean the wild mushrooms, making sure to remove any mud and dirt. Set aside on a clean kitchen cloth.

Place an ovenproof frying pan over a medium heat, add all the nuts and seeds and toast for a few minutes. Remove and place onto a board. Roughly chop and set to one side.

Add the onion to the same pan with a knob of vegan butter. Sweat for a few minutes, then add another knob of butter, the garlic and mushrooms. Cook for a couple of minutes, making sure the mushrooms don't crisp up too much. Remove from the heat.

In a food processor add the vegan breadcrumbs, along with the rosemary leaves, a pinch of salt and pepper and the fennel fronds and cranberries. Blitz for 30 seconds.

Melt the 100g measured vegan butter. Add the melted butter to the food processor with the toasted, chopped nuts and seeds and pulse for 5–10 seconds.

Add the parsley to the mushrooms. Sprinkle the nut and breadcrumb mixture over the top and toast under a grill until golden. Top with a few torn fennel fronds and serve.

roasted chickpea salad

The first time I made this I was staying in a gorgeous house in the hills of Ibiza. There wasn't much in the cupboards, so I just threw together what I had. I love the change in texture you get from roasting the chickpeas. It's like chickpea popcorn: lovely and toasted on the outside and fluffy on the inside. Baby kale is not as intense in flavour as adult kale, so it gives a lighter element to the dish. It's also easier to digest.

serves 4

½ tsp fennel seeds
½ tsp cayenne pepper
½ tsp smoked paprika
1 tbsp olive oil
1 × 400g tin of chickpeas
sea salt
270g cherry tomatoes
75g radishes
60g baby kale

FOR THE DRESSING
100ml classic vinaigrette
  (see page 240)
4 tbsp hummus

Preheat the oven to 180°C (fan 160°C/gas mark 4).

Mix all the spices with the olive oil in a bowl. Drain and rinse the chickpeas, drying them as thoroughly as possible. Mix the chickpeas with the oil and spices, season with salt and lay it all on a roasting tray. Bake in the oven for 30 minutes.

Meanwhile, slice the cherry tomatoes in half and thinly slice the radishes. Mix them both in a bowl with the baby kale.

In a separate small bowl, mix the vinaigrette with the hummus to make a dressing, then mix it through the salad.

Serve the salad on plates topped with the roasted chickpeas.

SNACKS

chapter 8

cheese 'n' greens quesadillas

Some of my best dishes are kind of whacked together. I love Mexican food. I used to love a famous Tex-Mex food chain in the US and this is my take on it using better produce. It's gorgeously gooey because of all the cheese, but it also has the greens for a bit of goodness. These are great with a cold beer.

serves 2

1 leek, chopped into 1cm (½in) half moons
80g tenderstem broccoli, chopped into 2.5cm (1in) pieces
2 green chillies, sliced
olive oil
sea salt
¼ tsp smoked paprika
200g Manchego cheese, grated
200g mild Cheddar cheese, grated
2 corn tortillas
4 spring onions, chopped
1 ripe avocado, de-stoned and sliced
zest of 1 lime
small handful of baby spinach leaves
juice of ½ lime
½ bunch of coriander, leaves only
1 red chilli, sliced
Cholula hot sauce and soured cream, to serve (optional)

Add the leek, broccoli and chillies to a small frying pan over a medium heat. Dry-fry for 1–2 minutes, then add a small glug of olive oil, a pinch of salt and the smoked paprika. Cook for 1 minute.

Mix both the grated cheeses in a bowl.

Heat a large non-stick frying pan over medium heat, then add one tortilla and sprinkle half the grated cheese on top. Add the charred greens evenly over the cheese and then add the spring onions, avocado slices, lime zest, a pinch of salt and the spinach.

Sprinkle with the rest of the grated cheese, then top with another tortilla. Fry for about 3–4 minutes until the cheese goes all gooey and sticks the tortillas together. Place a plate over the pan, flip the tortilla and toast the other side for 3–4 minutes.

Place on a board and cut into four pieces. Squeeze the lime juice over the top and sprinkle with the coriander leaves and the sliced red chilli.

Drizzle with Cholula hot sauce and soured cream, if using.

fried leftover
pasta cake

This is perfect for when you're drunk or hungover and want to use up what you have in the fridge. Squid ink spaghetti takes things up a notch but you can use whatever pasta you want. I first saw something like this being made on TV by Nigel Slater. I adore Nigel – he's one of my favourite chefs, and he describes food like no one else.

serves 2

50g Parmesan, grated
25g Cheddar cheese, grated
1 medium egg yolk
100ml double cream
1 tbsp olive oil, plus extra for frying
sea salt and black pepper
15g parsley, chopped, plus extra
    for garnish
200g leftover cooked spaghetti
3 sun-dried tomatoes, chopped
200g crème fraîche
browned shallot dressing, for drizzling
    (see page 236)

Mix the grated Parmesan and Cheddar in a medium bowl, along with the egg yolk, double cream, 1 tablespoon of olive oil, a pinch of salt and pepper, and the parsley. Mix thoroughly, then add the cooked spaghetti and combine it all together. Add the sun-dried tomatoes.

Heat a little olive oil in a medium frying pan over a medium heat. Add the spaghetti mixture and fry for a few minutes, turning over halfway through, until slightly crisp and golden.

Cut into two or four pieces and add a dollop of crème fraîche on each one. Drizzle with the browned shallot dressing and sprinkle with parsley. Serve.

hot apple and
pork sausage rolls

Everyone loves a sausage roll, don't they? They're part of British heritage. These aren't your average sausage rolls – the caramelized onion and chilli flakes liven things up and you've got that whole sweet and spicy thing going on. These are amazing at parties or else a great addition to a packed lunch, both for adults and kids.

makes 6–8

1 apple, grated

400g sausage meat, or sausages with the skin removed

1 tsp chilli flakes, plus extra for the top

½ bunch of chives, roughly chopped

1 tbsp honey

1 × 375g pack of puff pastry

1 medium egg

pinch of cayenne pepper (optional)

ketchup or brown sauce, to serve

Put the grated apple in a bowl along with the sausage meat. Stir in the chilli flakes, chives and honey. Mix until it all binds together and shape into a thick cigar.

Flour a work surface, then roll out the puff pastry with a rolling pin until about 1–2cm (½–¾ in) thick. Turn it so that the shortest side faces away from you. Lay the sausage meat cigar into the centre of the pastry, leaving 2.5cm (1in) of pastry on either side.

Preheat the oven to 180°C (fan 160°C/gas mark 4) and line a baking tray with greaseproof paper.

Beat the egg and brush it over the pastry. Carefully fold the pastry over using your fingers to lightly press and seal into a sausage roll shape.

Brush the roll with more egg wash and sprinkle with a few chilli flakes or a pinch of cayenne pepper.

Cut the ends off the roll, then slice into 6–8 portion sizes and place them on the lined tray. Bake in the oven for 35–45 minutes. When cooked, leave the rolls to stand for 10–15 minutes before serving with a dollop of ketchup or brown sauce.

prawn and lettuce cups
with charred pineapple

These are super light, and probably one of the healthiest recipes in my book. They're great for a barbecue and have a tropical feel to them. All of the ingredients are so easy to cook and the homemade chilli oil gives an extra kick. Serve as a quick starter or whenever people begin complaining that they're hungry.

serves 2

1 small pineapple, peeled and cored
   and chopped into 2cm (¾ in) slices
1 tsp cinnamon
140g raw tiger prawns
olive oil
sea salt and black pepper
1 × 300g romaine lettuce
drizzle of chilli oil (see page 234)
zest 1 lime
juice of ½ lime

Heat a griddle pan to searing hot. Cover the pineapple slices in a light dusting of cinnamon and griddle for 6 minutes on each side until charred and caramelized. Allow to cool, then roughly chop into chunks on a board.

Cover the tiger prawns in a glug of oil and a pinch of salt and pepper. Using the same griddle pan, cook the tiger prawns for 1–2 minutes on each side.

While the prawns are cooking, trim the lettuce by ripping the stems off. Lay the lettuce on a plate and place the prawns in and around the lettuce, along with the charred pineapple.

Drizzle on the chilli oil, lime zest and juice, and serve.

kickin' baked jalapeños

When I was twelve years old, my mum took me to New York for my birthday. I was obsessed with anything American, especially the candy (or sweets to you and me). I tried deep-fried jalapeño 'poppers' and they were amazing. I've made these a bit healthier and have baked them instead. These are in homage to that trip with my mum.

serves 5–6

200g large jalapeño peppers
280g cream cheese
sea salt
1 tsp smoked paprika
100g Cheddar cheese, grated

FOR THE CRUMB COATING
100g salted butter
25g coriander
200g breadcrumbs

Preheat the oven to 200°C (fan 180°C/gas mark 6) and line a baking tray with greaseproof paper.

Cut all the jalapeños straight down the middle, trying to keep the stalk intact as it looks good and makes them easier to pick up. I like my jalapeños spicy, so I leave the seeds in, but you can scrape them out if you wish.

Mix the cream cheese, a pinch of salt and the paprika in a bowl. Grate in the Cheddar cheese and mix everything together well with a fork.

Fill all the jalapeño halves with the cheese mixture (don't overfill) and scrape flat. Lay them on the lined tray.

To make the crumb coating, melt the butter and add to a food processor with the coriander and breadcrumbs. Pulse for 30 seconds.

Layer the breadcrumb mixture over each filled jalapeño.

Bake in the oven for 30–35 minutes or until golden on top and the cheese is melted and bubbling.

smoked salmon
and wasabi
cream bagels

This is a classic Jewish dish influenced by Japan. I was making a normal smoked salmon bagel one afternoon and I had some wasabi in the cupboard, which is basically Japanese horseradish. It just goes really well with salmon and adds a little twist. This shows you can be inventive with everything, even your bog-standard sandwich!

serves 2

1 small cucumber
sea salt and black pepper
20ml rice wine vinegar
2 sesame-seed bagels
4 tablespoons cream cheese
1 tsp wasabi
100g smoked salmon

Slice the cucumber lengthways with a peeler to create thin ribbons. Place them in a bowl and mix with a pinch of salt, a crack of pepper and the rice wine vinegar. Leave the ribbons in the acid of the vinegar for a few minutes to 'cook'.

Slice the bagels in half and toast.

Mix the cream cheese and wasabi together. Spread the mixture over the bagels and layer the salmon on top with a few slices of cucumber. Serve with the remaining cucumber on the side.

baked potato wedges
with chives, parmesan
and truffle

I made truffle fries when I was working at Ceilo restaurant in Miami
for Angela Hartnett. They were deep-fried so this is my healthier
take. Truffles are a luxury, so go for truffle oil instead if you prefer.
Everything here has strong flavours but they work really well and
don't overpower each other.

serves 4

6 medium potatoes
sea salt
olive oil
6 rashers of streaky smoked bacon
grated Parmesan, to serve
handful of chives, chopped
drizzle of truffle oil, to serve

Preheat the oven to 200°C (fan 180°C /gas mark 6) and line a baking tray
with greaseproof paper.

Cut the potatoes lengthways into wedges and rinse in cold water. Place them
in a large saucepan filled with fresh cold water. Season with plenty of salt
and bring the water up to the boil. Simmer for 20 minutes and then drain.
Allow the potatoes to cool and steam-dry for 5 minutes.

Mix a good glug of olive oil with a healthy pinch of salt. Coat the wedges
with the oil and place them on the lined tray, along with the streaky bacon.

Roast them in the oven for 20–25 minutes until golden and crisp. Put the
bacon and wedges in a bowl and cover in the Parmesan, chives, a pinch of
salt and the truffle oil.

*/ If you're feeling extra fancy,
you could slice fresh truffles over
the wedges.*

nduja devils
on horseback

I adore devils on horseback and I have done for years. And of course, my love affair for nduja continues. I am pretty sure that I'm the only one who has made this recipe with nduja, so it's become a signature dish. These are great for dinner parties, drinks parties, at Christmas; you can just push a cocktail stick in them and eat to your heart's content.

---

makes 20

10–12 rashers of streaky bacon
100g fresh nduja (or else from a jar)
1 tin of pitted prunes

SPECIAL EQUIPMENT
cocktail sticks

Preheat the oven to 200°C (fan 180°C/gas mark 6) and line a baking tray with greaseproof paper.

Start by laying the bacon rashers out flat on a chopping board and slicing them in half lengthways. Roll the nduja into pea-sized balls.

Drain the prunes thoroughly and add a ball of nduja to the centre of each prune. Place each prune at one end of each slice of bacon and roll over till you have a cigar shape. Stick a cocktail stick into the prune to hold it together.

Repeat until you've used all the bacon or prunes.

Place them on the lined baking tray and bake for 15–20 minutes, until golden, crisp on the outside and gooey and spicy in the middle. Serve.

DESSERTS

chapter 9

tamarind treacle tart

This is another classic with an Isaac Dirty Dishes twist. Tamarind is toffee-like but quite acidic, so it cuts through the treacle slightly and makes it just sweet enough. This reminds me of my childhood, when my mum used to make treacle tart. I'd eat it with vanilla ice cream or fresh cream, but choose whatever takes your fancy.

serves 6–8

200g plain flour
100g fridge-cold unsalted butter
sea salt
1 medium egg yolk
1 tbsp ice-cold water

FOR THE TREACLE FILLING
150g tamarind, shelled
450g golden syrup
80g fresh white breadcrumbs

SPECIAL EQUIPMENT
20cm (8in) round tart tin

Add the flour, butter and a pinch of salt to a food processor. Blend for 30 seconds until you get a breadcrumb-like consistency. Add the egg yolk and ice-cold water, and pulse for 10 seconds.

On a clean work surface, fold the pastry lightly and quickly into a ball. Wrap in cling film and allow to rest in the fridge for 30 minutes.

While the pastry is resting, make the tart filling. Place the tamarind in a medium bowl and pour 100ml boiling water over the top. Making sure it's not too hot, mash together with your hands to loosen the pulp, then pass through a sieve.

Using your fingers, remove the toffee-like pulp from the seeds and discard the seeds and any string.

Put a bowl over a pan of boiling water and stir together the golden syrup, breadcrumbs and tamarind pulp until warm and mixed thoroughly.

When the pastry has rested, preheat the oven to 180°C (fan 160°C/gas mark 4) and grease the tart tin.

Remove the pastry from the fridge and roll it out on a floured board into a large circle around 1–2cm (½–¾ in) thick. Carefully lower the pastry into the tin. Poke the bottom with a fork all over the base, then line with cling film and baking beans, rice or coins. Blind bake for 10 minutes, then remove the baking beans and cook the base for another 5–8 minutes.

Remove the baking beans and cling film and spoon in the treacle mixture. Bake the tart for 30 minutes until sticky, golden and set.

/ You can also use 100g shop-bought tamarind paste, but it gives a slightly more acidic flavour.

dirty chocolate cake

This is one of my signature dishes: a really basic chocolate cake recipe that's extra indulgent thanks to all of the chocolate sauce and delicious walnuts. It also looks really elegant with raspberry dust. This is a special take on a chocolate cake I've had on every single birthday since I was born – although this one hasn't got Smarties dotted on the top highlighting my age!

serves 8

100g unsalted butter
200g caster sugar
2 large eggs
3 tbsp cocoa powder
65g plain flour
seeds of 1 vanilla pod
80g milled walnuts
big handful of fresh raspberries
15g freeze-dried raspberry dust or
   whole freeze-dried raspberries

FOR THE ICING
70g unsalted butter, softened
200g milk chocolate
100g icing sugar
100ml double cream

SPECIAL EQUIPMENT
20cm (8in) cake tin

Preheat the oven to 180°C (fan 160°C/gas mark 4). Grease the cake tin and line with baking parchment, then grease the parchment on the sides of the tin.

Put a small saucepan of water on to boil. Set a heatproof bowl on top, then add the butter and allow to melt. Remove from the heat and add the sugar and eggs, then whisk together.

Add the cocoa powder, flour, vanilla and milled walnuts. Mix until combined.

Pour the mixture into the lined cake tin and bake for 15–20 minutes. Once the cake has baked and cooled, make the icing.

To make the icing, set another heatproof bowl over the boiling water in the pan and add the butter and chocolate. Let them melt together, then add the icing sugar and double cream. Whisk until smooth.

Spread the icing over the cake and top with the fresh raspberries and raspberry dust or freeze-dried raspberries.

spiced pineapple upside-down cake

The first time I ever had this was when I was working in Miami for Angela Hartnett. One of the other chefs was a good mate of mine called Mario, and when his mum found out I'd never had pineapple upside-down cake, she made one for me and Mario brought it into work. It was so sweet and delicious. I've redeveloped it and added the chilli because I like spices with my sweet!

serves 6–8

150g unsalted butter
150g caster sugar
1 tsp baking powder
150g self-raising flour
3 large eggs
1 tin of pineapple slices
1 red chilli
50–100ml dark rum
2 tbsp brown sugar

SPECIAL EQUIPMENT
23cm (9in) round baking tin

Place the butter and caster sugar in a bowl or the bowl of a stand mixer. Beat until white and fluffy, then add the baking powder, flour and eggs. Mix together until all combined, then set aside.

Preheat the oven to 180°C (fan 160°C/gas mark 4). Grease and line the baking tin.

Reserving the juices in the tin, place the pineapple rounds in one layer at the bottom of the lined baking tin.

Deseed the chilli, reserving a few of the chilli seeds for the syrup glaze. Slice the chilli into 1cm (½ in) rounds. Place a chilli slice in the centre of each pineapple ring. Carefully pour the sponge mixture over the pineapple and chilli and bake for 35–45 minutes, until cooked through.

Meanwhile, make the syrup glaze. Pour the pineapple juices into a saucepan over a gentle heat. Add the rum, the reserved chilli seeds and brown sugar. Mix together.

When the cake is cooked through, turn it out with the pineapple on top. Pour the glaze over the top while the cake is still hot, then allow the cake to rest and cool. Serve.

idiot's
eton mess

You can't go wrong with this. Eton Mess is basically a pavlova that has been dropped on the floor. It's an elegant mash of ingredients: chocolate, strawberries and cream. This one is so simple but it looks great. You can make it in advance for a dinner party, or throw it together at the end. Serve it on a huge plate at the table and just let everyone get stuck in with a few spoons.

serves 4

4 meringue nests
150g clotted cream
50–100g hazelnuts
100g dark chocolate
300ml double cream
½ tsp vanilla essence or
  seeds of 1 vanilla pod
6–8 ripe figs (240g)

Start by lightly crushing the meringue nests onto a large plate. Dot small spoonfuls of clotted cream in and around the nests.

Lightly toast the hazelnuts in a dry pan until golden, then crush lightly in a clean tea towel or pestle and mortar. Set aside to cool slightly.

Put a small saucepan of water on to boil. Set a heatproof bowl on top and melt the chocolate. Meanwhile, start whisking the cream in a separate bowl until you get soft peaks, then add the vanilla essence or seeds.

Cut the tops off the figs and quarter them. Lay half of them in and around the meringue and clotted cream.

Dollop the whipped cream and the rest of the figs around the plate. Scatter with the crushed hazelnuts, then drizzle the slightly cooled, melted chocolate on top.

rhubarb and apple crumble

I remember my godfather making this for me when I was fourteen. I love rhubarb, I wish it was available all year round. It's such a gorgeous pink colour and the taste is a mixture of sweet and sour. You sweeten it with sugar but it still retains that acidity. This is a traditional crumble topping because sometimes you shouldn't mess with the classics.

serves 8

700g cooking apples
juice of 1 lemon
800g rhubarb
200g sugar
seeds of 1 vanilla pod
custard or ice cream, to serve

FOR THE CRUMBLE
150g plain flour
150g rolled oats
150g brown sugar
2 medium egg yolks
pinch of sea salt

Preheat the oven to 180°C (fan 160°C/gas mark 4).

Peel and core the apples. Quarter and cut them into 2cm (³⁄₄ in) slices, then place into a bowl along with the lemon juice. Cut off the root of the rhubarb and discard. Cut the rhubarb into 5cm (2in) pieces, then pop in the bowl with the apples and cover in the sugar. Add the vanilla seeds to the bowl. Give it all a good mix together, then set aside.

To make the crumble, add all the ingredients to a bowl or food processor and mix together. You want a slightly wet, slightly crumbly mixture.

Transfer the fruit into a deep baking tray or ovenproof dish and crumble the mixture over the top.

Bake for about 1 hour, until the fruit is bubbling up the sides and the crumble is nice and golden. Serve with custard or ice cream; for me, custard always wins.

peanut butter and jam drop scones

These are so easy. You can knock them up in no time at all with just a few ingredients in your cupboard. They work with anything, although perhaps not Marmite! I've gone for jam, clotted cream and peanut butter. This is a great recipe to make with your kids. And lovely with a good cup of tea – a nice English brew of course.

serves 3–4

125g plain flour
25g caster sugar
¼ tsp ground cinnamon
1 tsp baking powder
1 medium egg
100ml whole milk
20g unsalted butter, plus extra
  for frying
pinch of salt

FOR THE TOPPING
1 tbsp crunchy peanut butter
1 tbsp strawberry jam
1 tbsp clotted cream
handful of toasted peanuts, crushed

Place all the dry ingredients into a medium bowl and mix. Whisk the egg and milk together in a small bowl and slowly pour into the dry mix, whisking as you pour. You're aiming for a fairly thick, smooth mixture.

Melt the butter and add to the mixture.

Heat a large non-stick pan and add a little butter. Drop in 1 tablespoon of the batter to form a scone, then add another two or three spoonfuls into the pan, and cook them for 3 minutes on each side, until golden. Transfer the scones to a plate and keep them warm while you make another batch. You should be able to make 6–8 drop scones from the mixture.

To serve, spread peanut butter over the scones, then add a dollop of jam and a spoonful of clotted cream. Top with the toasted peanuts.

dulce de leche semifreddo

This is another dish influenced by my time living in Argentina – I used to eat dulce de leche by the tub out there. I have such a sweet tooth. This version is Italy meets South America. Semifreddo is ice cream that hasn't been churned. It is a really super easy one to make as there's no baking involved. You just mix in a bowl, whack into a cake tin and freeze it. Slice it up when you're ready to serve.

serves 8

150g caster sugar
1 medium egg plus 3 medium
   egg yolks
seeds of 1 vanilla pod
450ml double cream
150g dulce de leche
handful of toasted hazelnuts,
   to serve (optional)
Alfajores or Biscoff biscuits,
   crumbled, to serve (optional)

SPECIAL EQUIPMENT
900g (2lb) loaf tin

Place the sugar, egg and yolks in a medium heatproof bowl. Add the vanilla seeds.

Put a small saucepan of water on to boil. Set the heatproof bowl on top and whisk the mixture together constantly for about 5–10 minutes until it thickens and turns almost white. Remove from the heat.

In a large bowl, whip the double cream until you have a stiff peak. Stir and fold in the sugar and egg mixture from the other bowl.

Prepare the loaf tin by lining it with high-quality cling film, or if you prefer you could double layer with normal cling film.

Pour half the cream mixture into the loaf tin and add half the dulce de leche. Make swirls into the semifreddo using a knife or toothpick. Top with the remaining cream mixture and cover tightly with the cling film so that no ice forms on the top. Leave to set in the fridge overnight.

When ready to serve, slightly heat the remaining dulce de leche in a small saucepan over a low heat. Turn the semifreddo out onto a serving plate and pour the dulce de leche over the top. Scatter on toasted nuts, or if you're feeling extra naughty, scatter biscuit pieces over the top.

'is this a dessert?' french toast and fried plantain

This is 'France meets Jamaica' in a dessert. French toast is so easy to make – it's basically fancy eggy bread. Plantain is used a lot in Caribbean cooking and I really like it. This dish is sweet on sweet. The spices add a nice warming element. It's also really cheap to make and doesn't involve much washing up.

serves 2

250ml whole milk
2 medium eggs
½ tsp ground cinnamon
½ tsp grated nutmeg
1 large plantain
coconut oil, for frying
50g butter
2 thick slices white bread
sea salt
maple syrup, for drizzling
zest of 1 lime

Mix together the milk, eggs, cinnamon and nutmeg in a large bowl. Whisk until combined, then set aside.

Peel the plantain and slice straight down the middle. Cut into four equal pieces.

Add a spoonful of coconut oil to a large pan over a medium heat. Add the plantain and fry for 3 minutes on each side. Around 30 seconds before they are cooked, add a knob of butter. Cook until golden then transfer to a plate and set aside.

Wipe the same pan clean with kitchen roll and bring to a medium heat. Soak each slice of bread in the batter until almost soggy, but still holding its shape. Add another knob of butter to the pan and cook each side for 1 minute, or until toasted and golden brown.

Cut each slice of bread in half and serve up, topped with a knob of butter and the plantain. Drizzle in maple syrup and top with the lime zest.

sticky toffee
loaf with rum

No Sunday roast is complete without a sticky toffee pudding, or in this case, a sticky toffee loaf. For me, this just shouts lazy Sundays: you've eaten your roast, been out for a walk, then you're on the sofa when the sticky toffee pudding comes out. You can buy ready-made ones but nothing beats making your own. Just don't overcook the base because it will dry it out – and no one likes a dry sticky toffee pudding! Serve with vanilla ice cream.

serves 4

200g medjool dates, de-stoned
  and chopped
1 tsp bicarbonate of soda
150g brown sugar
150g butter, softened
2 large eggs
150g self-raising flour
½ tsp cinnamon
½ tsp mixed spice
1 tbsp baking powder

FOR THE TOFFEE SAUCE
50g butter
250g Muscovado sugar
125ml double cream
1 double shot of rum

SPECIAL EQUIPMENT
900g (2lb) loaf tin or 23cm (9in)
  round baking tin

Preheat the oven to 180°C (fan 160°C/gas mark 4). Pop the dates in a bowl and cover with 400ml boiling water. Add the bicarbonate of soda and leave to soak and cool.

In a bowl or stand mixer, mix the brown sugar and butter together until light and fluffy. Add the eggs and whisk together. Next add the cooled dates and most of the liquid and whisk until combined. Finally, add the flour, cinnamon, mixed spice and baking powder. Mix until fully incorporated.

Next, line and butter the loaf tin or baking tin. I prefer to use a loaf tin for this recipe. Add the cake mixture and pop in the oven for 35–45 minutes or until the knife comes out clean.

While the sponge is baking, start making the toffee sauce. In a pan heat the butter and sugar together until melted, then add the double cream. Bring up to the boil then add the rum.

When the sponge is ready, dot with a few holes here and there. Pour half the sauce over the sponge while it's still in the tin and allow it to soak in for 15–20 minutes. Remove from the tin, slice thickly and serve with vanilla ice cream and the remaining sauce.

silly syllabub

Syllabubs were really popular in the sixteenth and seventeenth centuries. I don't want this dish to be forgotten – it is delicious and so easy to make. So let's bring back the syllabubs. This is where the English side of me meets my love of Italian ingredients. I love Amaretto and it gives a nice alcoholic punch to the syllabub. This feels like you're having a dessert and a stiff drink at the same time.

serves 2

1 × 284ml pot of double cream
juice of ½ lemon
zest of 1 lemon
50g icing sugar
50–100ml Amaretto liqueur
50g dark, sweet pitted cherries,
   chopped
4 Amaretto biscuits

Put two small cups or jars into the fridge to get cold.

In a large, cold bowl add the double cream, lemon juice and half the lemon zest. Sieve in the icing sugar and whisk until you get a soft, almost runny peak. Fold in the Amaretto liqueur.

Pop a handful of chopped cherries into each cold cup or jar. Layer the syllabub mixture over the top.

Crush the biscuits over the top and top with the remaining zest. Transfer to the fridge until ready to serve.

SAUCES AND DRESSINGS

chapter 10

SAUCES AND DRESSINGS

Introduction

Oils and dressings are just great to have in your arsenal. They make day-to-day life easier and they're so much better than the ready-made supermarket ones, which can be really sugary. I think dressings are very underrated because a good one can go a long way. You can use it on a simple side salad, or put it in a gravy, or in a sauce to liven it up. It's always good to have a few at hand and they keep for up to 3 months. If you're going to make just one, I would say it has to be my classic vinaigrette (see page 236). You can add different flavours to it, shake up the jar, take a bit out, add in some walnut oil, or shallots, or a bit of Dijon mustard … basically you can do anything with a classic vin. The others are all really versatile as well, for instance salsa verde (see page 240) is great on a chicken breast, or even if you're making a simple tuna sandwich. Whack a bit of salsa verde in and it will just take things up a level.

how to make mayonnaise

All you need to make fresh homemade mayo is a little bit of elbow grease and it will taste 100 times better than shop-bought; I promise it's absolutely worth the effort. It's a great sauce to have knocking about in your fridge.

makes 200ml

1 medium egg yolk
1 tsp Dijon mustard
1 tsp white wine vinegar
juice of ½ lemon
200ml vegetable oil
sea salt

Mix the egg yolk, mustard, vinegar and lemon juice in a medium bowl. Whisk them all together, then slowly and gradually add the oil, whisking continuously until you get a smooth, rich mayonnaise. Add a pinch of salt.

If you find it is a little thick, add a little water to thin the texture.

You can keep this in a tightly sealed container in the fridge for 3–4 days.

/ For jerk mayonnaise add 1 tablespoon dry jerk seasoning.

chilli oil

250ml light olive oil
1 whole large dried red chilli

Transfer the oil to a small saucepan and heat until it just starts bubbling. Add the dried chilli and turn down to a very low simmer. Cook for 20 minutes.

Remove the oil from the heat, then transfer to a sterilized glass bottle or jar. Squeeze the dried chilli into the bottle and use a funnel to carefully pour in the chilli oil. You can use straightaway, but I find if you wait a week you get a much better, rounder flavour.

You can keep the oil in the sealed glass bottle or jar for up to 3 months.

---

garlic oil

makes 250ml

250ml light olive oil
2 whole large bulbs of garlic, skin-on
   and bashed

Transfer the oil to a small saucepan and heat until it just starts bubbling. Add the bashed garlic and turn down to a very low simmer. Cook for 30 minutes.

Remove from the heat and let it stand for an hour for the garlic to infuse, then transfer to a sterilized glass bottle or jar. Strain the garlic oil as the garlic can turn unpleasant if left in the oil, then funnel or carefully pour into the jar or bottle. You can use straightaway.

You can keep the oil in the sealed glass bottle or jar for up to 3 months.

/ I sterilize old jars or bottles for storing the oils, or even the bottle the oil came in. Simply clean it and rinse with boiling water.

classic
vinaigrette

40ml white wine vinegar
120ml extra-virgin olive oil
pinch of sea salt
1 tsp smooth Dijon mustard

Pour everything into a jar, shake and serve. This is the base to loads of my vinaigrettes. You could use wholegrain mustard to change it up.

You can keep this in a tightly sealed container in the fridge for up to 3 months.

---

browned shallot
dressing

makes 170ml

4 shallots
olive oil, for frying
1 quantity of classic vinaigrette
  (see above)

Peel and slice the shallots down the middle, keeping the core intact, then chop them as finely as you can. Add a glug of olive oil to a small frying pan and add the shallots.

Cook on a low heat for about 20–25 minutes, stirring all the time so they don't catch. You want them a deep golden brown and nutty tasting, not fried and crisp.

Add them to a jar of classic vinaigrette (see above) and shake.

You can keep this in a tightly sealed container in the fridge for up to 3 months.

apple cider
vinaigrette

makes 250ml

60ml apple cider vinegar
1 tbsp smooth Dijon mustard
180ml extra-virgin olive oil
1 tsp dark brown sugar
juice of ½ lemon

Pour everything into a jar, shake and serve.

You can keep this in a tightly sealed container in the fridge for up to 3 months.

---

sweet garlic
dressing

makes 250ml

1 bulb of garlic
sea salt
olive oil, for drizzling
1 quantity of classic vinaigrette
   (see opposite)
1 tsp runny honey
1 tbsp chives, chopped (optional)

Preheat the oven to 180°C (fan 160°C/gas mark 4).

Cut the garlic bulb in half. Sprinkle with a pinch of salt and a little olive oil. Put the two halves back together and wrap tightly in tin foil.

Place in the oven for 40 minutes, then remove and allow to cool slightly.

Squeeze the sweet roasted garlic cloves out onto a board. Mush the cloves with a knife into a paste and stir into a jar of classic vinaigrette (see opposite), along with the runny honey. Add the chopped chives for a fresher taste.

You can keep this in a tightly sealed container in the fridge for up to 3 months.

spicy yoghurt and mint dressing

makes 500g

25g mint leaves
1 green chilli, deseeded and finely
  chopped
1 garlic clove, crushed
zest and juice of 1 lemon
sea salt and black pepper
500g natural yoghurt

Place the mint, chilli and garlic in a medium bowl or jar and stir. Add the lemon zest and juice and a good pinch of salt and pepper. Add the yoghurt and either stir or put a lid on the jar and shake it up.

You can keep this in a tightly sealed container in the fridge for up to 1 week.

---

salsa verde

makes 100g

50–100g bunch of parsley,
  leaves only
2 garlic cloves
6 anchovy fillets
2 tbsp cornichons
2 tbsp capers
1 tsp red wine vinegar
olive oil

Place the parsley leaves into a pestle and mortar or a small blender. Otherwise, you could chop this finely on a board if you don't have either.

Once you've blended or crushed the parsley, mix all the ingredients together and blend or crush them with a few glugs of olive oil.

You can keep this in a tightly sealed container in the fridge for up to 1 week.

dirty chilli sauce

makes 1 litre

500g red chillies
4 red scotch bonnets
olive oil, for drizzling and frying
6 garlic cloves
2 large onions
2 tsp garlic powder
3 tsp chilli powder
100g sugar
12 tbsp salt
2 × 400g tins of plum tomatoes
500ml white wine vinegar

Every household needs a go-to sauce for those lazy days when you just need to up the flavour. This dirty sauce packs a punch and keeps for up 3 months – if it will last that long!

Preheat the oven to 200°C (fan 180°C/gas mark 6).

Pick the green tops off all the chillies and discard. Mix both types together then divide into two portions. Transfer one half into a baking tray with a glug of oil and the garlic cloves. Roast for 30 minutes.

Top and tail the onions and place in a food processor, along with the fresh chillies and the roasted chilli and garlic. Blend for 1 minute.

Hit a large saucepan with a few glugs of olive oil and sweat the blended chillies and onions for 15 minutes. Add all the dry spices, sugar and salt and cook for a further 3 minutes. Add the plum tomatoes and mush in the pan with a fork.

Add the vinegar and 500ml water and simmer on low for 30 minutes.

Add everything to a blender and blend until smooth with a thick soup consistency.

Pour into clean, sterilized airtight jars or bottles. It will keep in the fridge for up to 3 months. You'll have loads, so why not seal the jars and give to mates as presents?

basic tomato sauce

Nothing beats a homemade tomato sauce. If you find yourself with a spare hour, get a big batch of the tomato sauce going; you can easily cool it down and freeze for another time.

makes 1 litre

olive oil, for frying
1 onion, chopped
2 garlic cloves, chopped
1 tbsp tomato purée
handful of parsley stalks
2 × 400g tins of chopped tomatoes,
   or 800g chopped plum tomatoes
sea salt

Add a big glug of olive oil to a large saucepan over a medium heat. Add the chopped onion and sweat for a few minutes, then add the garlic and sweat for a few minutes more.

Add the tomato purée and parsley stalks and cook for 2 minutes, before adding the tomatoes. Add 1 tin measure (400ml) of boiling water and bring the heat down to a simmer. Cook for 20–35 minutes depending on preferred consistency.

You can keep this in a tightly sealed container in the fridge for up to 1 week.

index

page numbers in *italics* refer to images

ABOUT THE AUTHOR

Isaac Carew

Isaac Carew's dad and godfather both worked in kitchens, so Isaac grew up washing mussels and leafy greens. In his teens Isaac trained at culinary school for two years before getting his big break in 2007, cooking alongside Angela Hartnett at The Connaught in London and El Cielo in Miami. Here his passion for homemade pasta grew.

In 2008, Isaac was spotted outside Selfridges and approached to become a model. He has fronted major campaigns for the likes of Hermès, Moschino and Valentino and been photographed by Rankin and Nick Knight.

Isaac lives in London.

ACKNOWLEDGEMENTS

The Dirty Dishes

I'd like to thank Hellie Ogden at Janklow & Nesbit for giving me the opportunity and direction to secure my first book deal, and to the amazing Carole Tonkinson and the team at Bluebird, Jodie Lancet-Grant, Jess Duffy, Don Shanahan and Martha Burley, for believing in me and understanding my vision for *The Dirty Dishes*. A huge thank you also to Grace and Louise at Independent Talent.

As someone with dyslexia (thank you dyslexia, for giving me creativity and imagination instead of perfect spelling!), I could never have dreamed of having my own cookbook, but here it is. The thing you're holding is the finished product, and I'm incredibly happy with it; I hope you enjoy using it as much I did writing it.

I'm deeply grateful to my father Andy for being the first to instil my passion for the food world, and for teaching me that *mise en place* (food prep before service) is key. I'd also like to thank Angela Hartnett for encouraging my honest and true love of Italian food – most of all, pasta. And to all the chefs I've met along the way, the mavericks and the truly talented.

And finally, to my godfather Scottie, my sister and family and all my loved ones (you know who you are), for having faith in me and always being there when I've needed you.

First published 2019 by Bluebird
an imprint of Pan Macmillan
20 New Wharf Road, London N1 9RR
Associated companies throughout the world
www.panmacmillan.com

ISBN 978-1-5098-4100-4

A CIP catalogue record for this book is available from the British Library.

Printed and bound in China.

Publisher Carole Tonkinson
Senior Editor Martha Burley
Senior Production Controller Sarah Badhan
Art Direction & Design Emma Wells at Studio Nic&Lou
Prop Styling Louie Waller
Food Styling Becks Wilkinson

Visit www.panmacmillan.com to read more about all our books and to
buy them. You will also find features, author interviews and news of
any author events, and you can sign up for e-newsletters so that you're
always first to hear about our new releases.